The Aposto

MW00929736

Preparing the church for the coming glory

by

Jeff van Wyk

Team Impact
publishing group

1st *Printing*

The Apostolic Anointing

Preparing the church for the coming glory

ISBN 978-1-477-64493-5

© 2012 Jeff van Wyk

Team Impact Christian University
5536 Superior Drive Suite D
Baton Rouge, LA70816
USA

Tel: 1 225 292 1771

www.tiuniversity.com

Published by:

Team Impact Publishing Group
5536 Superior Drive Suite D
Baton Rouge, LA70816
USA

Cover
Donné Roeloffze - thehours@hisoffice.co.za

*T*his book is dedicated to Dr Billy and Rentia Smook who are Emeritus Pastors of The Full Gospel Church of God, Benoni, South Africa. They have mentored many sons and daughters in the faith over many decades of faithful service to the Lord. My wife Marlene was saved under their ministry and they continue to be a great source of inspiration and blessing to our ministry.

Table of Contents

Introduction

The apostolic anointing is about to usher in a new church that will be different to any church that has ever existed before from the birth of the first church two thousand years ago.

This anointing will bring a renewed focus on equipping and maturing believers so that they will fulfill the prophetic mandate in this last generation of the church age.

A unique move of God's Spirit is coming that will see the apostolic anointing restore the hearts of God's children to the Father.

Malachi 4:5-6 - Behold, I will send you Elijah the prophet Before the coming of the great and dreadful day of the Lord. And he will turn The hearts of the fathers to the children, And the hearts of the children to their fathers, Lest I come and strike the earth with a curse.

This revival will release the glory of God upon the church in a physical manifestation of heavens' power and love and the sons and daughters of God will perform mighty works which will exceed anything that has ever been done by the 1st century church apostles.

The harvest is plentiful and the purpose of this revival is to bring millions and millions of people from every nation into the Kingdom of God.

It will be different to any move of God that the church has experienced in the past. God is about to raise up modern day apostles who will preside over this revival and organize the church into a strong well-disciplined army which will be ready to do battle. No force will be able to withstand the advance of God's people.

Hosea 6:1-3 - Come, and let us return to the Lord; For He has torn, but He will heal us; He has stricken, but He will bind us up. After two days He will revive us; On the third day He will raise us up, That we may live in His sight. Let us know, Let us pursue the knowledge of the Lord. His going forth is established as the morning; He will come to us like the rain, Like the latter and former rain to the earth.

Not everyone will be part of this revival and not every church will experience God's glory. Only those who have been preparing their hearts in total commitment to Him will see His glory. Those who have been crying out to God "I want to see your glory" will see His glory. I am amazed to discover how few Christian leaders believe in the end time revival.

God is calling us to holiness and separation from the world. God is calling His leaders today to preach an uncompromised Word and to begin equipping the saints in earnest anticipation of the coming glory. This will not be another revival that will come and then fizzle out again. It will have a purpose and that is to bring God's people into the full stature of Christ and to evangelize the nations.

This glorious new church will come into unity and will no longer be concerned with doctrinal and political agendas. They will be absolutely absorbed into the tangible visible presence of the Lord. It will bring people together from every part of society who will love God and worship Him and demonstrate genuine love towards each other regardless of race, gender, class, or reputation.

This church will no longer be laughed at by the world because of its immoral standards, disunity, fallen leaders, greed for money, and so on. The apostolic anointing will empower leaders who will be fearless and will not be intimidated by anyone. They will boldly proclaim the Word without compromising or watering down the truth in order to make it socially acceptable. There will be a clear dividing line between truth and error.

The revived church in this generation will not comprise of people who only go to church for an hour per week wanting to be entertained. The doors will be open every day and the true believers will remain in God's presence. They will submit willingly to the leaders who will begin to prepare them for battle.

It is time for God's people to draw close to Him. We must be able to accurately discern the times and seasons and plan our lives accordingly. God wants us to draw closer and closer to Him every day, to sacrifice the things of the flesh, and to walk earnestly in the Spirit. This concerns the rest of our lives on earth which will extend into eternity. Do not miss this moment. Let this be your motto as you begin to enjoy your spiritual inheritance:

Joshua 24:15 - And if it seems evil to you to serve the Lord, choose for yourselves this day whom you will serve, whether the gods which your fathers served that were on the other side of the River, or the gods of the Amorites, in whose land you dwell. But as for me and my house, we will serve the Lord."

Revival is coming! You cannot have it both ways. Let those who want to be religious and lukewarm continue without the anointing. But you do not have to be like that especially if you want to be part of God's great plan. Fall in love with Jesus again. Give Him everything.

Your life is precious in the sight of God. Who will you give it to? Make your choice today and do not delay for the time is short, the apostolic anointing is coming, and the harvest is ready for your message of hope, love, and salvation. The anointing upon your life is about to be expanded throughout the earth.

Romans 10:18 - But I say, have they not heard? Yes indeed: "Their sounds has gone out to all the earth, and their words to the ends of the world."

Walk continually in the Spirit and do not walk out of step with God by walking in the flesh. Be quick to repent.

Make good choices for your life and you will see how God will begin to bless you and use you for His plans and purposes.

God bless you

Dr Jeffrey W. van Wyk
Team Impact Christian University

5536 Superior Drive Suite D
Baton Rouge, LA70816 USA

Tel:1 225 292 1771

dean@tiuniversity.com
www.tiuniversity.com

June 18, 2012

Chapter 1

Understanding The Apostolic Anointing

Jesus and His church

We can never study the apostolic anointing without looking at Christ's relationship with His church. The apostolic anointing is driven by a great love that the Lord has for His church.

> *Ephesian 5:25-27 - ......just as Christ also loved the church and gave Himself for her, that He might sanctify and cleanse her with the washing of water by the word, that He might present her to Himself a glorious church, not having spot or wrinkle or any such thing, but that she should be holy and without blemish.*

Jesus is passionate about the church and paid the highest price by shedding His own blood for the church.

Song of Solomon 4:7 - You are all fair, my love, And there is no spot in you.

Throughout the ages, Jesus has been building His church. That has been His main purpose since the 1st century inception of the church. It has always been an apostolic function and the Lord has built His church by means of the apostolic anointing.

Psalm 127:1 - A Song of Ascents. Of Solomon. Unless the Lord builds the house, They labor in vain who build it; Unless the Lord guards the city, The watchman stays awake in vain.

Matthew 16:18 - I will build My church, and the gates of Hades shall not prevail against it.

Before we can study the function of apostles in the church, we must understand that Jesus is the source of the anointing and anyone who wishes to operate with an apostolic anointing must be connected with Jesus Himself. The Bible teaches us that Jesus Christ is "The Apostle" because He was sent by God the Father.

Hebrews 3:1 - Therefore, holy brethren, partakers of the heavenly calling, consider the Apostle and High Priest of our confession, Christ Jesus.

Jesus was the Sent One, the Apostle, and High Priest of our confession.

A need for the apostolic anointing

There is a great need for anointed leaders in the church today who will walk intimately with the Lord and follow His agenda to transform the church into the beautiful picture that we have of Christ's bride.

Ephesians 5:27 - That He might present her to Himself a glorious church, not having spot or wrinkle or any such thing, but that she should be holy and without blemish.

This is a futuristic or prophetic picture of the church and we are clearly not there yet. At the moment we can see so many spots, blemishes, and ungodliness. The church as we see it today can be described as:

- Divided
- Defeated
- Mocked
- Poor
- Struggling
- Ineffective
- Compromised
- Confused

But praise God, things are going to change in the near future because Jesus is about to release an apostolic anointing upon the church and it is going to be transformed into the image of Christ. God is going to touch the church supernaturally and the apostolic anointing will do the supernatural work necessary to bring about this transformation.

God is going to raise up a new breed of leaders who are not known. They are alive on the earth today but have not yet been revealed. They are His best kept secret in these last days. He has hidden their identity but they are about to be revealed and will release their apostolic anointing upon the church.

The true apostolic ministry has not yet been fully revealed and is the prophetic expectation that the church is looking for. The fact that certain Christian leaders are appointed as apostles or carry the title of an apostle, does not necessarily imply that they are functioning in the full anointing of an apostle.

Although many apostles today are planting churches and fathering many congregations, the apostolic anointing is primarily needed to bring the church into maturity, unity, and likeness of Christ. The church is about to be transformed by the Spirit of God so that it can be ready for the purpose that God has for the church in this season. The bride will match the Bridegroom in power, perfection, beauty, and glory. That is the mandate of the apostolic ministry.

The seven churches

Revelation 1:18-20 - I am He who lives, and was dead, and behold, I am alive forevermore. Amen. And I have the keys of Hades and of Death. Write the things which you have seen, and the things which are, and the things which will take place after this. The mystery of the seven stars which you saw in My right hand, and the seven golden lampstands: The seven stars are the angels of the seven churches, and the seven lampstands which you saw are the seven churches.

Before we study the miracle transformation of the end time church, let us look at the journey that the church has taken over the past 2000 years.

In the book of Revelation chapters 2 and 3, Jesus addresses seven churches that existed in the 1st century. They were the seven major churches of early Christianity. Jesus speaks directly to them and unambiguously admonishes these churches and highlights their good and bad attributes.

Jesus addresses His concerns to the pastors and spiritual leaders of these churches and we conclude from His words that the churches were definitely not perfect.

The seven churches were located in:

1. Ephesus
2. Smyrna
3. Pergamon
4. Thyatira
5. Sardis
6. Philadelphia
7. Laodicea

It has been pointed out by church historians that these messages applied to progressive stages of church history and that the seven churches of Revelation 2 and 3 represent the condition of the church during the various periods comprising the 2000 year church era. In this particular order, they cover the entire history of the church. Whereas the Book of Acts covered the first 30 years of the church, the Book of Revelation takes it from Acts to the present time.

1	Ephesus	Apostolic age	Before AD 100
2	Smyrna	Age of Persecution	100 to 313 AD
3	Pergamos	Imperial Church Age	313 to 590
4	Thyatira	Age of Papacy	590 to 1517
5	Sardis	Sardis Reformation Age	1517 to 1730
6	Philadelphia	Missionary Age	1730 to 1900
7	Laodicea	Age of Apostasy	1900 to today

Jesus speaks to us about these churches and points out their strengths and weaknesses.

	Church	Strengths	Weaknesses
1	Ephesus	Busy Hates evil	Lost their first love Too many programs Lots of activities
2	Smyrna	Persecuted Prosperous	
3	Pergamos	Faith is strong	Worships idols Sexually immoral Doctrines of demons Compromises
4	Thyatira	Good works Faithful Patient	Corrupt leaders Abuse of power Sexually immoral
5	Sardis	Alive	Complacent Slothful Prayerless Religious Imperfect
6	Philadelphia	Perseveres Commended	
7	Laodicea		Elitist Comfortable Own strength Has need of nothing

The churches in Smyrna and Philadelphia are the only two churches that Jesus commends by adding no negative statements. The church in Laodicea is criticized the most and attracts no positive comments from the Lord. Sadly, this church relates to the church in which we find ourselves in today and this is surely not the church that will represent the body of Christ when Jesus returns.

The eighth church

We have studied the strengths and weaknesses of all seven of the churches throughout history.

We must concede that the church has achieved a lot throughout the ages. It has preserved the Word of God, evangelized the nations, brought millions upon millions to salvation, kept the faith, and preserved the anointing of the Holy Spirit throughout its history. But it has also been guilty of many failures and imperfections. When we study the prophetic end of the church, we have to agree that the church has not yet transformed into its intended image of perfection.

Ephesians 4:7-16 - But to each one of us grace was given according to the measure of Christ's gift. Therefore He says: "When He Ascended on high, he led captivity captive, and gave gifts to men." (Now this, "he ascended"-what does it mean but that He also first descended into the lower parts of the earth? He who descended is also the One who ascended far above all the heavens, that He might fill all things.) And He Himself gave some to be apostles, some prophets, some evangelists, and some pastors and teachers, for the equipping of the saints for the work of ministry, for the edifying of the body of Christ, till we all come to the unity of the faith and of the knowledge of the Son of God, to a perfect man, to the measure of the stature of the fullness of Christ, that we should no longer be children, tossed to and fro and carried about with every wind of doctrine, by the trickery of men, in the cunning craftiness of deceitful plotting, but, speaking the truth in love, may grow up in all things into Him who is the head-Christ-from whom the whole body, joined and knit together by what every joint supplies, according to the effective working by which every part does its share, causes growth of the body for the edifying of itself in love.

Ephesian 5:25-27 - ...just as Christ also loved the church and gave Himself for her, that He might sanctify and cleanse her with the washing of water by the word, that He might present her to Himself a glorious church, not having spot or wrinkle or any such thing, but that she should be holy and without blemish.

Song of Solomon 4:7 - You are all fair, my love, And there is no spot in you.

When we study these passages it is quite evident that the church is about to change supernaturally. Some of the positive characteristics of this glorious church are as follows:

- In full unity of the faith
- Perfect
- Reflects Christ's image
- Sanctified

- Cleansed
- Glorious
- Without spot
- Without wrinkle
- Without blemish
- Mature
- Works together effectively

When we look at these prophetic images of the church we can only conclude that the seventh or Laodicean church described by the Lord is not the last church that will be on earth when Jesus returns. Another church will come after the seventh church which is the eighth and last church. This church is about to manifest on the earth and will be birthed in power through the apostolic anointing which is about to be poured out.

This church has never existed before and will rise from the ashes of the previous seven churches and grow into the full stature of Christ and will perform mighty works in the name of Jesus. This church will be anointed with power and each member will do their part in the body working together in unity to establish God's plan in the last days.

Today the body is doing its own thing and really needs to pull itself together and function as one body.

Prophetically, the eighth church is different from the seven churches and although they shared common weaknesses, the seven churches were not all the same.

What should the church look like? It should look like Christ. When the church looks at itself in the mirror it should see Jesus. It must not see division, strife, or envy, and it must definitely not see the image of the world. Today the church looks like the world. When the body comes into the fullness of Christ it will be unpopular with the world. When the body comes into its fullness it is going to be at enmity with the world. The world is going to hate its fullness and just as the world hates Christ it is going to hate the church as well.

To summarize all this, the restoration of the apostolic anointing to the church will bring the church back to the Biblical pattern. The restoration of the apostles will bring the necessary stability to the family of God that fathers and mothers bring to natural families.

When the apostles are restored to the church, the five-fold ministry will be complete and the apostolic anointing will flow and bring divine order to the house of God. The church will come into the fullness of God's power and anointing that will be needed to meet any challenge and bring in the harvest at the end of the age.

The church is going to emerge out of its cocoon and it is going to be the beautiful bride that represents Christ and will be ready to be joined to the Bridegroom.

The church is going to transform into a beautiful bride. A bride normally looks beautiful on her wedding day. The church may not look all that good at the moment, but the best is still to come out of the church. The church is going to rise, wash her face, anoint her head, and make herself beautiful.

The ministry gifts

After Pentecost, the first prophetic voice was that of Peter who, basing his prophecy on the prophet Joel, proclaimed that there would be an outpouring of God's Spirit in the last days which would be similar to that experienced at Pentecost.

Peter's prophecy differed to that of Joel.

Joel 2:28 - And it shall come to pass afterward that I will pour out My Spirit on all flesh...

Acts 2:17 - And it shall come to pass in the last days, says God, that I will pour out my Spirit on all flesh...

After Pentecost, the apostolic ministry was birthed. The message of the gospel was preached everywhere and churches were established.

We are living in the last days and eagerly await the outpouring of the apostolic anointing on the church which will initiate and complete its perfection.

1. The Five-fold ministry

To understand the function, purpose, and calling of the present day apostle, we must first have an understanding of the five-fold ministry.

Ephesians. 4: 11-12 - And He Himself gave some to be apostles, some prophets, some evangelists, and some pastors and teachers, for the equipping of the saints for the work of ministry, for the edifying of the body of Christ.

Jesus gave the five-fold ministry gifts to the church. They are still valid and needed in the church today. These gifts have not been taken back but will continue until every believer comes into unity and reaches the level of maturity and perfection of Christ Himself.

In order for the church to come into full unity and perfection, it will need all five of the ministry gifts of Christ. That means each one will be involved in this function. The apostolic anointing will flow when all five offices are fully restored.

It will need apostles, prophets, pastors, teachers, and evangelists working together and all doing the same thing with their individual anointings. They will equip God's people for the work of the ministry and prepare each believer to fulfill their ministry and calling.

These ministry gifts will therefore continue in the church and will be in full operation until Jesus comes back for His perfect and completed bride.

When Jesus was on earth He fulfilled every function of His ministry. However, when He returned to the Father, He gave these gifts to men for the completion of the work He had begun.

In His life and ministry, Jesus expressed all five of these ministry gifts and gives an expression of Himself to the church in the form of these ministry gifts.

The five-fold offices cover all the leadership ministry activities of Christ while He was here on earth and each one expresses the corresponding aspect of Jesus. For example, the apostle is the expression of Jesus as an apostle in that person and the prophet is the expression of Jesus as a prophet in that person, etc. The full expression of the ministry of Jesus requires the full five-fold ministry to be in operation in the church today.

a. Apostle

Hebrews 3:1 - Therefore, holy brethren, partakers of the heavenly calling, consider the Apostle and High Priest of our confession, Christ Jesus.

Jesus was the Sent One, the Apostle, and High Priest of our confession. He is the One whom we confess.

b. Prophet

Matthew 21:11 - So the multitudes said, "This is Jesus, the prophet from Nazareth of Galilee."

Jesus functioned fully in the five-fold office of a prophet. Since it is Jesus who has given this gift to the body of Christ, the prophet should manifest the same qualities that Jesus displayed when operating in the prophetic anointing.

c. Pastor

John 10:11 - I am the good shepherd. The good shepherd gives His life for the sheep.

Jesus was the Good Shepherd which is the same word for pastor in the Greek translation.

d. Evangelist

Isaiah 61:1 - The Spirit of the Lord is upon Me, Because He has anointed Me To preach the gospel to the poor.

Jesus was an evangelist and preached the gospel of the Kingdom.

e. Teacher

Matthew 9:35 - Then Jesus went about all the cities and villages, teaching in their synagogues.

Jesus spent a large portion of His ministry teaching and explaining Scripture from the age of twelve.

The Bible clearly demonstrates that God makes a call on individuals and appoints them. The Holy Spirit then sends them out to fulfill their individual ministries and confirms their anointing. This principle is true for the five-fold offices even though a vast majority of church leadership have achieved their offices through other means.

The five-fold offices are given to the body of Christ by Christ as a gift. It must be clearly understood that a gift is not earned. For this reason, these five-fold offices cannot be earned. No one can appoint another person into these positions. The Holy Spirit may use the church leadership to confirm the call of God on an individual but they cannot decide to appoint a person into any one of the five-fold ministries.

The ministry gifts are appointed by God and not by the choice of men. Unlike the Old Testament, this gift is not inherited from one generation of a particular family to the next. The genealogy regarding spiritual inheritance finished with Christ. For this reason there are no recorded inheritances of the anointing from any of the apostles to their children.

The five-fold ministry gifts of Jesus to His church are not founded upon the Law. Jesus gave new gifts under grace instead of under the Law which now includes the Gentiles also.

It is the combined task and function of all five of these ministry gifts to bring the body of Christ into unity by working together and all five will function in the apostolic anointing which will equip the saints for service and bring the body of Christ to maturity. The church today has certainly not come into full maturity and unity of faith which proves that the five-fold ministry still needs to be fully established in the body of Christ.

The five-fold ministry can and should work together, while each does their own ministry and fulfill their individual gifting.

Christ is the head of His church and it is He alone who determines who is called into any of the five-fold gifts.

Each person is divinely endowed with the spiritual gifts necessary to carry out that calling. All the offices of the five-fold ministry have different functions and are for different purposes and are to be performed by people who are chosen and anointed by God.

The church needs every function of the five-fold ministry gifts which Jesus has given to His church, but sadly very few Christians recognize all of them. Recognition is very important if the church is to benefit from these gifts.

Each of the five offices carries its own unique anointing and has its own individual work. For these ministries to work together to accomplish the building up of the body of Christ, they must recognize their differences and be yielded and submitted to one another. They are each directly responsible to the Lord Jesus Christ and are directed by the Holy Spirit to do this work.

Just as the human body has five senses for its protection and care, God has provided five ministry gifts for the protection and care of the body of Christ.

2. Foundational ministries

Ephesians 2:20-22 - Having been built on the foundation of the apostles and prophets, Jesus Christ Himself being the chief cornerstone, in whom the whole building, being joined together, grows into a holy temple in the Lord, in whom you also are being built together for a dwelling place of God in the Spirit.

The apostles and prophets are the two foundational ministries in the body of Christ.

Jesus revealed Himself as the cornerstone of the church. But He continues to build it through His apostles and prophets.

1 Corinthians 12:28 - And God has appointed these in the church: first apostles, second prophets.

Apostles are the first and prophets are second among the ministries in building the church of God because they lay a foundation of understanding concerning the mystery of Christ.

Unfortunately, these are the two ministries that are least recognized in the church today. But God is bringing order back to His church and is fully restoring the ministry of the apostles and prophets.

Without the ministry of apostles and prophets the revelation of the blueprint necessary for the building is incomplete.

The prophet works closely with the apostle as they lay a foundation and bring strength and order to the body of Christ. God has given His grace to apostles and prophets to receive a revelation of His mysteries and to reveal them to the body.

When we look at the current state of the church, it is clear that it needs to make significant foundational shifts and changes. It is evident that the ministry gifts of the pastors, evangelists, prophets, and teachers are active in the church today. But when we make a comparison of where the church should be headed in terms of its maturity and unity, the office of the apostle has not been fully restored to the church. The bride of Christ can only prepare for the Bridegroom once all five of these anointings are fully active.

> *Ephesians 4:7-8 - But to each one of us grace was given according to the measure of Christ's gift. Therefore He says: "When He ascended on high, He led captivity captive, And gave gifts to men."*

3. The hand

The five-fold ministry represents the hand of God working in the church today. This is the hand that performs the work that He desires in the world today.

The fingers of the hand symbolically represent the five-fold ministry that God sets up within the church. The hand feeds, cares for, and washes the entire body. The hand needs all the fingers and its thumb to be effective in its work. The church needs all five of its ministry gifts if it is going to be effective.

The five-fold ministry equips all the other ministries and it is they who do the work.

The ministry gifts serve to reveal the plan of God. The apostles, prophets, evangelists, pastors, and teachers are like fingers stretching out. They must learn to balance one another out and work together in order to get the task done.

a. The thumb represents the apostle

The apostle is the thumb because it is the only finger that can touch all the others and grip. It therefore establishes, completes, and brings order to the other ministries.

The thumb is obviously different to all the other fingers of the hand. The thumb is solid. It is shorter, fatter, and blunter and set in the hand very differently to the other fingers. In fact all the other fingers, although different to one another, have vast similarities and are all basically the same when compared to the thumb.

The thumb is set in the hand in such a way that it can interact with all of the fingers and oppose them as well and keep them in line when needed. But the thumb is however too blunt and short to do the delicate work required in the palm. But it can certainly keep a close watch on all activities and all the fingers within the palm. The thumb is also the closest to both the heart and the head.

b. The forefinger represents the prophet

The forefinger or index finger is the one that points, shows the way and directs. The index finger represents the prophet who points the way and warns.

c. The middle finger represents the evangelist

The middle finger stands out from among the rest and reaches out to save the lost. It is the longest and besides the thumb, the strongest finger and is supported on all sides by the other fingers.

It has the longest reach of all the fingers and can reach out the furthest to hook in and draw in others into the palm of the hand, where the whole hand clasps them and ministers to them.

d. The ring finger represents the pastor

The ring finger represents the pastor, because that finger is associated with love, caring, and faithfulness.

The pastor is symbolically married to the sheep and is always with them. This symbolizes the marriage between Christ and the church.

e. The little finger represents the teacher

The little finger balances the rest of the hand and represents the teacher. It is the smallest finger, the shortest and thinnest, and the only one small enough to clean out the ears.

The little finger is almost separate from the rest of the hand, but is perfectly placed on the outer edge of the hand to catch those who are falling out of the palm of the hand. It is very important and is often needed to bring people back into the hand.

If the little finger lets go the grip is severely weakened. Though seemingly small and insignificant, the little finger is designed specifically for digging into inaccessible places.

f. Relationship between each

The apostle works best with the prophet. The index finger is closest to the thumb. The apostle and prophet work closely together and form the foundational ministries.

The index finger is closest to the middle finger. The prophet works closely with the evangelist as well.

The pastor is located between the teacher and the evangelist. These are the two the pastor works best with. One wins souls, the other trains them. The pastor oversees the process. A shepherd leads his sheep.

The evangelist is between the prophet and the pastor. Someone has to take in the new babes and feed them and shepherd them. The pastor and teacher are well equipped for this. The prophet provides insight for the evangelist and helps keep things pointed in the right direction. They hear from God and reveal His heart and purpose for the hour, not just the future.

The little finger cannot function or work on its own. It is interesting to note that the ring and little finger are almost inseparable When the one moves the other moves in near unison.

The teacher works really well alongside the pastor, but not the evangelist or the prophet. They mostly benefit the pastor and the congregation.

Chapter 2

The Six Anti-Types

Unless we understand the apostolic call on the church today we could miss God completely. There are so many things that are set up in opposition against God's end time plan. The devil knows that his time is short and he is using every resource that he can to frustrate God's Kingdom and sadly, he also uses the church to work against what God wants.

> *Zechariah 3:1   Then he showed me Joshua the high priest standing before the Angel of the Lord, and Satan standing at his right hand to oppose him.*

We need to understand that the devil is set up to oppose and embarrass us before God. Everything that God does and every good thing that He releases upon the earth, is opposed by the kingdom of darkness.

The word "anti' means "another way" or "opposition". These six oppositions or six anti's are directed by Satan against the Kingdom of

God and many times we find that the church is complicit in working against the anointing of God. We need to be aware of this so that we can test what we are doing and ensure that we are working with God and not unwittingly against Him. God does not want His church to work against Him but to work with Him.

The entire kingdom of darkness is set up to oppose the Kingdom of God and it is violent, consistent, well structured, and very well planned. The devil will use people in the world to carry out his evil plans and if he can, he will use Christians as well.

Having knowledge will give us power against the enemy especially in these last days. The church needs to have an apostolic spirit which will enable it to expose these plans. An apostolic church is a church that lives in a heavenly environment.

God is calling His church to live in heavenly places with Him. God does not want the church to be programmed whereby they come to church on a Sunday, do everything else on a Monday, and by Tuesday He is forgotten. God wants us to love Him with our whole heart, mind, and soul and this includes our possessions, our time, and our heart. Every word that comes out of our mouths should glorify God. That is an apostolic mind-set. In these times in which we are living, God is going to call the church to operate in a new dimension of the anointing. We are either going to represent what God wants in this time or we are going to represent what the devil wants.

God is challenging the church in this season because He does not want us to be lukewarm and indifferent. He wants us to be apostolic by having a Kingdom mind-set which is a twenty four seven walk with the Lord.

The apostolic church is the true church and it loves Jesus. It is a church that is totally sold out to God. God wants you to be totally sold out for Him. God does not want to share you with anyone. He wants all of you.

The devil has been defeated but he is not out of commission yet. Every war that is fought has two conflicting sides and it generally means that one side will lose. The devil is behind all these conflicts and when one side loses, the devil does not care. His aim is simply to steal, kill, and destroy. He does not care who wins or who loses, as long as he can cause as much bloodshed and destruction as possible. After the devastation, he simply moves on to the next bloodbath. Although one nation may be defeated by the war, the devil is not. He simply moves onto another conflict.

But Jesus said it is going to be worse in the last days because nations will rise against each other and there will be conflict everywhere. We can see that happening with new wars breaking out almost every day.

Satan is the one trying his utmost to destroy nations because he is not out of commission yet. He is still very busy and that is why God wants us to be actively involved in His church to oppose him.

What is the definition of spiritual warfare? God gave me a very simple definition. Anything that advances God's Kingdom and pushes back Satan's kingdom will initiate a spiritual war because it invokes the wrath of the devil. Anything you do that God loves and Satan hates, will involve you in spiritual warfare because it hurts the devil. When you pray, you are engaged in spiritual warfare, because it is directed towards God. When you become involved in a church and you start growing spiritually, those actions are acts of warfare against the enemy. Instructing your children in the things of God is spiritual warfare.

If you want to come against the devil and you want to win in this fight, do everything that God loves. But understand that there is a war out there. Do not play with the devil.

An apostolic church does not preach compromising messages that tickle the ears of the people. An apostolic message is one that aggressively challenges the people and their lifestyles so that they can be moved by the Spirit of God to make much needed changes in their Christian conduct.

Today we see so many people wandering from church to church seeking feel-good messages but the true apostolic church will never preach these messages. We are living in serious times and God is not going to build His army with people who are not totally committed to His cause.

God is about to pour out an apostolic anointing which will cause the church to rise to the full stature of Christ. God's heart is not for the church to represent anything that does not look like Christ.

1. The anti-Father

John 14:6 - Jesus said to him, "I am the way, the truth, and the life. No one comes to the Father except through Me.

Mankind has always been searching for God but Jesus is the only way to the Father. False religions believe that there are many ways to God and do not believe that Jesus is the only way. Jesus is therefore the one stumbling block to a single world religion, because Christians know that without Jesus there is no salvation, no eternal life, and no relationship with the Father and they will not accept that there can be another way.

The devil knows that if he can take you away from a father he will ensure your demise. He has worked tirelessly to mess up the definition of "father" throughout the past generations and has done this to ensure that people struggle to relate to a father figure that typifies the heart of our Father in heaven.

The devil has done this by trying to destroy fathers in the family. He has been active in destroying marriages so that children do not grow up with a father in the home. Today, fathers are not raising their children. They have been driven from their home through failed marriages which has its true root in the devil's hatred of his Father. The devil hates marriages. He hates a father and a mother raising up their children together and sadly, he has not only been successful in the marriages of unsaved people, but has been very successful in destroying the marriages of born-again Spirit-filled children of God. The statistics for both groups are the same.

His aim is to destroy the righteous offspring of Godly men and women and tries to ensure that resultant generations of the righteous do not relate to God the Father. This spirit is called anti-Father because everything the devil does is against the Kingdom of God. He rebelled against his Father and uses that same strategy to convince the righteous sons and daughters to rebel against their fathers on earth.

There are young boys that are being raised up without their fathers in the home and they are so confused because there is no father to mentor them and where there is no father, the devil will ensure that someone else mentors that boy. He will be taken away from his God-given destiny and taken to the wrong places. The devil will ensure that someone will raise up that child who hates God and loves the devil.

If you are a father, set your home in order and make sure your family stays together. If you are a mother, do everything in your power to make sure your husband does not leave your home. When the devil targets your marriage, be aware that he is actually after your children and your children's children. Do not give him any opportunity or foothold into your home.

Joshua 24:15 - But as for me and my house, we will serve the Lord."

2. The anti-Son

The Bible tells us that anyone who is anti-Son is antichrist. The antichrist is coming to exert great influence on the earth for a time. But the antichrist is actually a demon spirit in the world that represents everything opposite to who Jesus is, what He has done, and what He desires. The antichrist opposes who Christ is.

1 John 4:3 - And every spirit that does not confess that Jesus Christ has come in the flesh is not of God. And this is the spirit of the Antichrist, which you have heard was coming, and is now already in the world.

If any person or religious group does not confess that Jesus Christ has come in the flesh, they do not promote heaven's agenda.

There are many that believe in Jesus and will openly admit that He was a great prophet sent by God, but they do not believe that He is God and the only way to God. There is no other way to God except through Jesus and to be anti-Son is to declare another way. That is the spirit of the antichrist.

This Laodicean spirit also works within the church and ensures that God's people have a lukewarm attitude towards the things of God. The church has lowered the standard of holiness and feed the people with feel-good messages that do not confront or challenge the lifestyles of the people.

This spirit also seeks to tie the church with other religious groups that do not believe in Jesus in a misguided belief that all religions should work together regardless of religious beliefs. To fit in they try their best not to allow their belief in Jesus to offend others. They are reluctant to speak about Jesus because their religious peers seek unity by declaring that all roads lead to God. It is a church that is afraid to confront anyone in case it loses popularity with the community.

The greatest attack against the church is coming from within the church by its leaders who are watering down the Word and making the Christian walk easy and casual without any need for lifestyle changes or taking responsibilities.

It is high time that the church defends the name of Jesus because if we do not have Jesus, we do not have God. If we do not have Jesus, we do not have eternal life. That is the message of the church and anyone who minimizes this position is under the influence of the spirit of the antichrist and is anti-Son.

The apostle Paul confronted everyone in defense of Jesus and he was not even intimidated by kings and rulers. He stood before them and refused to compromise. If we do not oppose government, they will pass laws that will violate our Christian values. They will trample on our religious freedom and even go as far as to instruct us how we should run our homes.

The apostolic church is one that influences the decisions that Governments makes.

What God do you serve? If it is not God the Father, God the Son, and God the Holy Spirit - the three in one God - then it is another god.

3. The anti-Word

A person who is anti-Word knows what the Bible says but does not apply it. These are people that oppose the Word of God. I find that people who try and make excuses or explain away the truths of God's Word, really do not want to obey what God says and they are usually the beneficiaries of their convictions. In other words, they stand to gain the most by not applying the Word. They do not want to obey the Word because it will mean that they will have to give up certain things, or it may cost them something.

For example, people who argue that it is not important to belong to a church are usually those who justify why they are not submitted to a church. You will never find someone who is benefiting from a relationship with their local church making such statements.

People who do not submit to the instructions and wisdom of the Word are deceived by the devil because he does not want them to live a full and abundant Christian life.

2 Timothy 4:3 - For the time will come when they will not endure sound doctrine, but according to their own desires...

This spirit is becoming more and more evident in these last days and many are being driven away from the church and away from

God because they do not want to submit to God's Word.

Every false doctrine, false religion, and cult today, is known as such because they have taken the pure Word of God and changed it. They do not even have to change it much to corrupt it. If we are not grounded in God's Word, we will be caught up in false doctrines.

There are so many people making sacrifices for their religions and their beliefs, but all God wants from us is to obey His Word. God teaches us that obedience is better than sacrifice.

4. The anti-Holy Spirit

Ephesians 4:30 - And do not grieve the Holy Spirit of God, by whom you were sealed for the day of redemption.

The anti-Spirit prevailing in the world is really messing up churches. When God's power and leading is rejected in favor of church programs, personal charisma, and abilities, it can grieve the Spirit of God.

The true apostolic church is led by the Spirit of God and allows God to move supernaturally in the meetings. Today, the anointing has been replaced by hype and other counterfeits which ensure that God's will is not accomplished.

God does not look at our flesh because flesh cannot bring glory to God. God is looking for weak vessels of clay that He can fill with His Spirit so that we can do supernatural things that give Him glory.

Moses was a person who could not speak properly because of a speech impediment, yet God used him to bring many powerful messages to Pharaoh.

The apostolic church knows that it does not qualify to do the mighty works of God in the natural or in the flesh. It understands that it needs God's power to be able to accomplish the impossible in cities, communities, and nations. The apostolic church performs signs and wonders and prays for those wanting to be filled with the Spirit. It prays for the sick and believes that God still perform miracles in and out of the church through anointed men and women of God.

Today, that simplicity has been replaced by sophisticated methods which brings a false order into the church. In so many churches today, the Holy Spirit is not welcome. Leaders fear that the presence and manifestation of the Holy Spirit can ruin their "successful" churches, but they are actually deceived by the anti-Spirit that is "churching" communities, but not transforming them by the power of God's Spirit.

Zechariah 4:6 - So he answered and said to me: "This is the word of the Lord to Zerubbabel: 'Not by (man's) might nor by (man's) power, but by My Spirit,' Says the Lord of hosts.

The only way we can be instruments in the hands of God to build God's Kingdom, is to allow God's Spirit to empower us. Everything we do should not be by our own ability, but by God's Spirit. When we perform spiritual things without God's Spirit, we grieve the Holy Spirit and this can bring great destruction and judgment upon the church.

How do we grieve the Holy Spirit? By not listening to the voice and leading of the Spirit. The Holy Spirit still speaks today and has a lot to say to the church.

1 John 2:27 - But the anointing which you have received from Him abides in you, and you do not need that anyone teach you; but as the same anointing teaches you concerning all things, and is true, and is not a lie, and just as it has taught you, you will abide in Him.

The Holy Spirit will teach you things that others do not know. There are secrets that the Holy Spirit has for your life and your ministry and when you make Him your friend, you will never ever be at a disadvantage.

5. The anti-ministers

Matthew 24:24 - For false christs and false prophets will rise and show great signs and wonders to deceive, if possible, even the elect.

Jesus has given us the five-fold ministry to build His church which is the ministry of the apostle, prophet, pastor, teacher, and the evangelist. Satan organizes his Kingdom in opposition to God's Kingdom and just as we have the true five-fold ministry operating in the church, there can also be the false five-fold ministry.

a. False apostles - There are false apostles that are setting themselves over the work of

God but who have not been sent by God. They are manipulating the church and leading people to the wrong place. I am not saying that every person who calls themselves an apostle today is a false apostle. There are those who carry an apostolic anointing by planting churches and looking after networks of churches. But the true office of the apostle is still to be fully restored, as they are going to be used by God in the last days to work with the other ministry gifts to bring the church to perfection and maturity.

b. False prophets - The Word tells us that we are living in a time of false prophets and we are warned not to listen to them. We need a discerning spirit in these days to make sure that we listen to the right people. It is becoming more and more difficult today.

c. False teachers - There is coming an attack against the church by false teachers and we should not listen to them. They are the ones who are corrupting the pure Word of the Lord and leading God's people astray. They will express their own opinions and deviate from the standard of the Word.

d. False pastors - The Bible tells us that false pastors will scatter the sheep but true pastors will love the sheep and look for the ones who are lost.

e. False evangelists - A false evangelist will draw people to themselves whereas a true evangelist will draw people and communities to Jesus.

The Bible tells us that some men and women in the five-fold ministry will stand before Jesus one day and will be rejected. Even the miracles they performed will not count in their favor. How frightening to think that there are men and women ministering signs and wonders in the name of the Lord who will be rejected by the Lord. We need to be so careful who we follow these days. We can only have certainty by walking closely and intimately with the Spirit.

6. The anti-church

The true church is an apostolic church. An apostolic church is one that is led by God's Spirit and builds God's Kingdom without any fear or intimidation. It is a church that is not moved by the opinions of others, but boldly and fearlessly proclaims the message of God for this season. It is a church that does not compromise God's standard of holiness and preaches the pure Word of God. It is not a popular church and probably does not fit in too well with the religious establishment.

It is a church that is embarrassing to its peers because it is radical. It is a church waiting for a fresh touch from heaven and knows it must stand ready for new instructions from the Lord Jesus Christ in the coming season.

It is a church that provides a safe spiritual haven for God's people and leads them to safety and protection. With them, there is no middle ground. It is all for God or all for the devil.

Revelation 3:14-16 - "And to the angel of the church of the Laodiceans write, 'These things says the Amen, the Faithful and True Witness, the Beginning of the creation of God: "I know your works, that you are neither cold nor hot. I could wish you were cold or hot. So then, because you are lukewarm, and neither cold nor hot, I will vomit you out of My mouth.

False churches are those that operate in the middle ground. As someone once said, the church has become so worldly and the world has become so churchy. The lines between the church and the world should be distinct, but the dividing lines have become so blurred that it is difficult to distinguish them from the world.

The anti-church spirit is one that causes churches to deviate from God's true pattern and life of the church. The false church tries so hard to fit in with society and prefers to be social rather than life-changing. Churches today spend so much money making their buildings comfortable and draw people who have become fat with feel-good messages but do not know the difference between hot and cold or what is wrong or right.

Chapter 3

God's Purposes For The Earth

A vicious battle is being waged for the souls of men and women in the spirit realm. It is a battle between God and Satan and the outcome will determine whether the truth of Jesus and His Lordship will reign in a person's life, or whether the deception of Satan will triumph.

Mankind is caught in the midst of a spiritual war with the Kingdom of God and Satan and his demons on the other.

Jesus Christ inspires believing Christians to dedicate themselves to the extension of His Kingdom throughout the world. Satan tries to seduce people to follow him for the extension of his demonic kingdom.

The devil seeks to corrupt and destroy individual believers, churches, cities, and even entire nations. His ultimate intention is to destroy the work of God and lead the whole world in rebellion against God. Satan goes "to and fro" in the earth and walks up and down in it.

Job 1:7 - And the Lord said to Satan, "From where do you come?" So Satan answered the Lord and said, "From going to and fro on the earth, and from walking back and forth on it."

1 Peter 5:8 - Be sober, be vigilant; because your adversary the devil walks about like a roaring lion, seeking whom he may devour.

The earth seems to be the special field of his activity. Satan and his host of spirit beings perpetrate their evil among people on the earth.

He operates in his own children and he operates against the children of God. These are the two spheres in which Satan functions.

Being destined to eternal hell, the devil wants nothing more than to bring human beings to join him in his own eternal damnation.

Satan offered Christ the kingdoms of the world in return for worship. This was a valid offer as the world was under his dominion.

From the fall of Adam until the advent of Christ, Satan was given a dispensation to bind the nations. That is why Satan was able to offer Christ the kingdoms of the world during the temptation in the wilderness. Jesus did not correct Satan about his offer but simply refused him.

Satan is the god of this world and greatly influences the actions of human beings. Subject to God's overruling power, he is allowed to strike at nations and influence the behavior of earthly rulers. God clearly shows that Satan sets fallen spirits over various worldly governments and they exercise great influence and power over their activities. The devil also uses civil authority to war against the followers of Christ. Christians today are engaged in the same manner of spiritual warfare that Jesus and His disciples confronted.

Revelation 13:7 - It was granted to him to make war with the saints and to overcome them. And authority was given him over every tribe, tongue, and nation.

The Bible shows that God desires all His children to grow in character and power and to conform to the image of Jesus Christ.

Because of their potential to grow more like Jesus and to advance the Kingdom of God, those who follow Jesus are under greater demonic attack than unbelievers.

God has always been leading His children and instructs us prophetically how we should live and how we should prepare and position ourselves in this season. We are a prophetic people and should speak forth the purposes of God in this generation.

God does not do things alone and has always used His servants on the earth to work with Him in order to establish His Kingdom on the earth.

The Bible is very clear that the earth is God's treasured possession and His plan is to establish heaven on earth. Satan presides over the atmosphere and forms a wall between heaven and earth.

He wages a fierce and relentless battle for control of the earth and has used every resource available to him to establish his kingdom on the earth. But he suffered a humiliating defeat at Calvary which limited his authority because of Spirit-filled men and women of God. He has done so much to steal the anointing and ability from God's children by enticing them into a comprised lifestyle.

There is an ongoing war between God's Kingdom and Satan's kingdom and this war is fought for the hearts and minds of people who are living on the earth. The conflict for each and every individual only ends when they die. God has enlisted us to work and fight with Him to limit Satan's influence of the earth until judgment day.

We need to understand that we will either be used by God for His purposes or by the devil for his purposes. There is no neutral ground. We are either for God or for Satan.

Our lifestyle and passion will either serve God's agenda or Satan's agenda. When you make a decision for God and apply all your resources to building His Kingdom, you are waging a war with God against His enemy.

Throughout history God has presided over the earth and has always enlisted men and women in every generation to work with Him to fulfill His plan for the earth. That is why Jesus gave us authority over all the works of the devil. In these last days, the fight is intensifying with great evil manifesting in our generation that has never been seen in any previous dispensation.

The devil is using strong distractions that is stealing the quality of life from men and women. One of his most powerful distractions is games and gadgets that keep our generation in a fictional world of cyberspace. I am not against the internet because it is a wonderful invention that provides so many benefits. But Satan is using cyberspace to create a counterfeit invisible or spiritual realm which aims to supplant the spirit realm that God created and which connects our spirits with God's Spirit. Instead, millions upon millions of people are becoming engrossed and lost in cyberspace connecting with fictitious people, false relationships, and demonic soul ties. Through these means, demons are setting up idols and receive worship which is due only to God.

There are people who spend every waking moment in cyberspace connecting intimately with individuals they perceive as a potential partner, but they have no idea who that person is or whether that person even exists.

There are a number of things Christians need to know.

1. Satan binds the nations

Throughout the ages, the devil has placed chains and burdens upon nations and he binds them up. Some examples of these bondages are religion, politics, poverty, and lawlessness. But God has revealed Himself as the bondage breaker.

Isaiah 14:24-27 - The Lord of hosts has sworn, saying, "Surely, as I have thought, so it shall come to pass, And as I have purposed, so it shall stand: That I will break the Assyrian in My land, And on My mountains tread him underfoot. Then his yoke shall be removed from them, And his burden removed from their shoulders. This is the purpose that is purposed against the whole earth, And this is the hand that is stretched out over all the nations. For the Lord of hosts has purposed, And who will annul it? His hand is stretched out, And who will turn it back?"

Satan is the bondage maker but God is the bondage breaker. God is using anointed men and women who are submitted totally to Him to be bondage breakers so that nations can be set free.

2. The purpose of man

Exodus 9:15-16 - Now if I had stretched out My hand and struck you and your people with pestilence, then you would have been cut off from the earth. But indeed for this purpose I have raised you up, that I may show My power in you, and that My name may be declared in all the earth.

During our lifetime on earth, we can achieve so much and accumulate many material things. But the only thing that moves God is to what extend we make ourselves available to Him. Our purpose is to give ourselves to the Lord completely and work with Him to build His Kingdom.

3. The two-fold purpose of Jesus

Jesus had a two-fold purpose while He was on the earth.

1 John 3:8 - For this purpose the Son of God was manifested, that he might destroy the works of the devil.

Firstly, God used Jesus in the frontline of the spiritual conflict on earth and He effectively set people free from sickness, oppression, and demonic possession.

Luke 4:43 - But He said to them, "I must preach the Kingdom of God to the other cities also, because for this purpose I have been sent."

Secondly, Jesus brought salvation and hope to the world through His death and resurrection. But note the order in which this was done. He effectively bound the strongman when He triumphed over the devil in the wilderness, and for three and a half years He plundered the devil's goods by casting out demons, raising the dead, and healing the sick. During this time He taught people by showing them the true picture of heaven. After His mission was accomplished, only then did He go to the cross to die for mankind.

4. The secret service

Through his intimate relationship with the Holy Spirit, Paul was able to ascend into heaven and access the blue print for the church and through this divine revelation, he revealed God's secret plan for Jews and

Gentiles alike as contained in God's New Covenant plan. Because he had access to intimate details of God's secret plans, Paul preached the good news to the Gentiles. In every generation, God has His special men or women who are given the secrets of heaven and who ensure the survival of that generation.

Initially, Jesus stood against the kingdom of darkness on His own. But now He has a mighty army of blood washed, Spirit-filled followers who are pushing back the kingdom of darkness.

Ephesian 3:10-11 - To the intent that now the manifold wisdom of God might be made known by the church to the principalities and powers in the heavenly places, according to the eternal purpose which He accomplished in Christ Jesus our Lord.

God is looking for those who will engage Him in faith and intimacy so that He can reveal His secret plans that can place His children in a strong position and have an advantage over the enemy. So much of the New Testament was written by Paul and these writings contain the mysteries of God that had never been revealed to any generation before and which equips and prepares us today for the greatest confrontation that is about to take place on the earth.

5. Power to the people

Acts 10:38 - How God anointed Jesus of Nazareth with the Holy Spirit and with power, who went about doing good and healing all who were oppressed by the devil, for God was with Him.

The purpose of the baptism in the Holy Spirit is to empower believers for Christian service what enables them to live a life of victory over the enemy.

The baptism in the Holy Spirit gives us the same possibilities of relationship to the Father and power in ministry as Jesus had on earth. God wants us to move into these possibilities. The baptism in the Holy Spirit is for all believers. This is a free gift and most times manifests itself in the speaking of tongues.

This power sets God's people apart from everyone else. It makes us more than conquerors through Christ Jesus. It gives us the ability to preach the gospel convincingly that will open up the eyes of those who are spiritually blind. It is not our power but His power. The same power that defeated Satan in his quest for total dominion on the earth is the power that lives within us. It is the same power that will make us excel and enable us to be more than victorious in every situation that we may face. It is the same power that raised Jesus from the dead. That is the power that lives in us!

Acts 1:8 - But you shall receive power when the Holy Spirit has come upon you; and you shall be witnesses to Me in Jerusalem, and in all Judea and Samaria, and to the end of the earth.

We have been given the upper hand because God has placed His power and ability within us

• • •

and He enables us to defeat His enemy and causes him to flee. The same power that Jesus used to defeat the devil is now available to every born again child of God.

Through His Spirit we are able to do the works of Jesus and when we operate in unity, we are able to do so much more for God.

6. He saves the best for last

God is revealing and releasing His purposes on the earth today and has saved the best for last. He has chosen us to be part of the greatest showdown ever. This battle started at the rebellion but you and I are called to finish it with God. We are the fresh troops. Those that have gone before us fought faithfully and tirelessly, but we are the fresh troops. God has called us uniquely in our generation and we will accomplish more than any other generation before us.

This generation represents those who have the best minds, the best hearts, and the best abilities to understand God's end time plan because God has kept the best generation for last. We will be part of the last showdown on earth.

God has given us a two-fold purpose and that put simply, is to bind and to loose.

Matthew 16:19 - And I will give you the keys of the kingdom of heaven, and whatever you bind on earth will be bound in heaven, and whatever you loose on earth will be loosed in heaven.

Mark 3:27 - No one can enter a strong man's house and plunder his goods, unless he first binds the strong man. And then he will plunder his house.

Only true Christians have this power and authority to bind and loose in the name of Jesus.

Jesus explained that believers must first bind the strongman before they can plunder his house.

This inherited authority as children of God must be used to bind the evil forces involved in any battle. All opposing powers, principalities, wicked rulers, and evil spirits must be defeated. The strongman must be bound before plundering the devil's kingdom. After that believers can loose or call forth God's plans for restoration, freedom, and deliverance.

That is how Jesus conducted His ministry on earth. After He was anointed at the Jordan, He was led by the Spirit into the wilderness and fasted for forty days. When He was at His weakest physically, Satan tempted Him three times. Jesus confronted him with the Word and after the third failed attempt, Satan left Him. The strongman was bound which opened the way for Jesus to plunder his goods which He did by casting out demons and healing the sick. He effectively loosed the blessings and power of heaven onto earth.

Faith in God's Word releases the power from heaven that binds evil by forbidding and declaring its activities unlawful. When something is loosed on the earth, its activities and presence are permitted and declared lawful.

God wants us to loose the bondages and the chains on cities, communities, and nations in the name of Jesus. As the true church rises in maturity, unity, and power, it will loose God's plans on the earth for the nations and they will be set free and receive Jesus. God's people will bind the strongman presiding over nations and then go in and break the chains off them. God is the bondage breaker and God has raised us up in this season to be His instruments of war. Through this apostolic anointing, we will be expanded to the ends of the earth and we will release heaven's blessings onto the nations. God has good plans for the earth and for all the peoples of the earth who will receive the message of the gospel.

No one in the upper room at Pentecost could have predicted how the revival would be packaged. When it came, there were manifestations that were never experienced before. For example, everyone spoke in other tongues.

There is coming a new move of God which is going to birth the church in power and will take it to every people group on earth. But we cannot really predict how this move will be packaged. The important thing is that we must recognize it when it comes. Just know that He is going to use us to fulfill His plans for this final generation and we need to be preparing our hearts and our minds so that we do not miss Him. He is going to come in a different way and not the way we perceive Him to come.

• • •

That is how the Jews missed their Messiah when He arrived in Bethlehem as a new born baby.

We must be very careful because God can come in any place, way, or form and we will be able to recognize Him if we are in the Spirit.

Everything will work out well for God's children in the last days. That is what Paul has taught us. Stop worrying about finances because God is your provider. Stop worrying about sickness and diseases that will come upon the world. He is your healer and your health. Do not worry about anything. God will be with us and we will be walking and working with Him in these closing days.

Romans 8:28 - And we know that all things work together for good to those who love God, to those who are the called according to His purpose.

Chapter 4

The Restoration Of All Things

The true Biblical meaning of restoration is:

- to bring back to a former or original condition from one of change or decay
- the act of renewal, revival, or re-establishment
- restitution of something taken away or lost
- something that is renovated

The ultimate restoration is the renewal of the church from its present condition into the image and majesty of Christ through the transforming power of the Holy Spirit. The restoration of all things will be initiated through the apostolic anointing that is about to be released upon the present day church. The church will be actively involved with Christ in restoring all things.

Matthew 17:11 - Jesus answered and said to them, "Indeed, Elijah is coming first and will restore all things."

Jesus spoke prophetically to His disciples and they asked Him questions about the end times. They had a prophetic desire to understand where Jesus was going with His church and they wanted to know more.

When we speak about all things it means everything in heaven, on earth, and under the earth, whether spiritual or physical. It is those things that can bring glory to God.

At present it is obvious that not everything glorifies God, but we are living in a time where God is about to restore all things and we are part of God's restoration plan. He does nothing without His children on earth and is busy building His Kingdom through us and with us. He is partnering with us and is not ahead or behind us, but walks in step with all those who walk in the Spirit and are following His blueprint.

God is restoring all things that will glorify Him. The church is going to come to a place where it will glorify God. We are not there yet but God's glory is coming back to His house and to His people. People will know us by the glory of God upon us and Jesus is restoring the full glory, relationship, and fellowship that we can have with Him.

We see in the Word that Jesus spoke prophetically of the spirit of Elijah that will come upon the church in the last days. It is going to be an apostolic anointing that will empower us to work with God to restore all things in heaven and on earth.

Malachi 4:5-6 - Behold, I will send you Elijah the prophet Before the coming of the great and dreadful day of the Lord. And he will turn The hearts of the fathers to the children, And the hearts of the children to their fathers, Lest I come and strike the earth with a curse.

God is going to pour out a fresh anointing upon His children in these last days which is going to bring about the restoration of His church. We are going to do mighty works with God through this anointing and we are going to work with Him to restore all things so that the earth will reflect the glory of heaven.

Acts 3:19-21 - Repent therefore and be converted, that your sins may be blotted out, so that times of refreshing may come from the presence of the Lord, and that He may send Jesus Christ, who was preached to you before, whom heaven must receive until the times of restoration of all things, which God has spoken by the mouth of all His holy prophets since the world began.

Times of refreshing are coming to God's people and to His church. These prophetic Scriptures give us a view of God's plan for the church from Pentecost to where we are today. All those who love God and who are alive on the earth today will be used for the restoration of His Kingdom. This generation is not like any other generation that has lived before. It is a unique generation and these words are given to us prophetically and through revelation so that we can prepare ourselves for the greatest move of God that has ever come on the face of the earth.

God is going to place His glory upon the church and His fire in our hearts and we are going to work with Him in this restoration process. What a wonderful privilege! We are living in exciting times.

We are living in times of deception where the counterfeit is very evident on the earth today. The devil is trying very hard to make the church not look like the church should look so that God's people do not represent what heaven is and do not represent who Christ is. But that is all about to change and the church will be restored in the image of the Bridegroom. Believers will become mature and will grow up and will come into the fullness and stature of Christ through the apostolic anointing.

We are right at this point in God's time line. When Christ manifests Himself, the antichrist will also manifest himself. The antichrist represents everything that opposes what Jesus stands for. The Laodicean church is the church that has been evident in the past 100 years. It is the lukewarm compromising church that Jesus spoke about when He described the characteristics of the seven churches and adequately describes the present-day church.

Revelation 3:14-16 - "And to the angel of the church of the Laodiceans write, 'These things says the Amen, the Faithful and True Witness, the Beginning of the creation of God: "I know your works, that you are neither cold nor hot. I could wish you were cold or hot. So then, because you are lukewarm, and neither cold nor hot, I will vomit you out of My mouth.

It is the last church that would exist historically over a two thousand year period from Pentecost. When we read about this last church, it seems as if the church ends in weakness and defeat. But the church does not end there. The Bible tells us that Jesus is coming for a glorious church without spot or blemish. This is the eighth church that will be birthed from the ashes of the Laodicean church. It will be the final church of the church age and will do mighty works upon the earth until Jesus returns.

When we look at the church today we can become quite discouraged. Today people are moving around looking for the prefect church but become disillusioned because they cannot find it. They go from church to church but cannot find the church that reflects Christ in the true sense. That is because the prefect church does not exist. It will not come about until the apostolic anointing has been released.

The church will become the beautiful picture of Christ's true bride and will work with Him to restore all the things that Satan has corrupted and destroyed.

The restoration of the true church

Haggai 2:9 - 'The glory of this latter temple shall be greater than the former,' says the Lord of hosts.

This is about to manifest. The time is closer than we think and not everyone will experience it. No one will experience this revival if they are not expecting it. God does nothing without revealing His plans to His prophets beforehand. Those who do not know what is coming will not receive what is coming. This revival is for the church and those who are not positioned for this move will not see it.

Today the church has become a leadership institute with motivational preaching. But this is not the purpose of the church and certainly not God's plan for it. The restoration of the church will reveal a new breed of leaders with an apostolic anointing who will boldly and fearlessly equip the believers and structure the church so that every member will go out and do great and mighty things. The restored church will expose the false church by virtue of its visible glory.

Why did Moses see the glory of God? He asked God to show him His glory and God gave him what he asked for. This is a prophetic prayer that we should be praying. The church will no longer be a weak institution but will be powerful and will represent Christ in every way.

There are nations that are bound by religion, politics, lawlessness, materialism, and many other bondages that hinder the people to come to Christ. But these chains will be broken when they see the glory and they will know that they have met with the true and only God.

Prophetically, the whole earth will be filled with the knowledge and glory of God. How will that come about? Those flames will be ignited in every nation by God's body of believers who will enter every nation with boldness and determination.

There are so many people today, including Christians, who really believe that the whole earth will be under the power of the antichrist. Yes, the whole world today is under his influence and he will exercise even more authority and power in the coming days. However, he is limited because of his defeat at Calvary and is subject to Christ's power which has been delegated to us. He may be able to come against defenseless people and nations, but he cannot overcome God's anointed warriors on the earth.

Revelation 11:15 - Then the seventh angel sounded: And there were loud voices in heaven, saying, "The kingdoms of this world have become the kingdoms of our Lord and of His Christ, and He shall reign forever and ever!"

The restoration of the Word

Today the Word is no longer the truth because so many church leaders have changed the Word to suit their own beliefs and the lifestyle and demands of the people. Messages are preached from pulpits around the world by church leaders who openly deny the deity of Christ, the virgin birth, the resurrection, and many more fundamental beliefs that have been held sacredly for the past two thousand years. The church has moved away from Christ's church to the people's church and reflects more and more the wishes of the people rather than what God requires of His children.

But God is about to restore the true church and will restore the truth of His Word. It will no longer be corrupted but will reflect His will for mankind and they will willingly submit in total obedience to what He wants.

Acts 2:42 - And they continued steadfastly in the apostles' doctrine and fellowship, in the breaking of bread, and in prayers.

The apostles' doctrine is not the doctrine of man, but the doctrine of Jesus and represents the truth. It is a doctrine that has not been corrupted by or subject to interpretation by man but reflects everything that God is and what He requires from His children. It is the roadmap that leads us to life with the Lord. The apostle's doctrine will once again be applied to the restored church and God's children will spill out onto the streets and preach the gospel.

False teachers and prophets do not come from outside, but come from within the ranks of the church. These leaders have great influence and are used very cleverly and effectively by the devil to deceive God's children, leading them away from their inheritance and eternal life.

God is about to restore His Word that will expose these lies and will once again be released as a pure source of living water that will refresh and nourish the people of God and bring them into unity and maturity.

The restoration of our relationship with God

Daniel 11:32 - Those who do wickedly against the covenant he shall corrupt with flattery; but the people who know their God shall be strong, and carry out great exploits.

There are so many Christians who know about God and know the Scriptures but have never met Him in a personal way. God is looking for those who will engage Him in love and intimacy. He wants to reveal Himself as a loving Father and longs to share the secrets of heaven with His children. Love opens up the secret treasure of heaven that can transform the earth.

God is about to restore this relationship and reach closer in a new refreshing way by imparting His love into the hearts of the men and women who have been serving Him faithfully.

He will enter their homes and their private sanctuaries and wrap His arms around them and transfer the love of a true father which will touch hearts and open eyes. People will want to serve Him more passionately because of these precious encounters with Him.

We cannot love people if we do not love God and we will not be able to go to nations without a love for them. Jesus left heaven and came to earth because He loved people. We will not be able to leave our hometowns and go to foreign lands if we are not powered by love.

God knows this and He is about to demonstrate His love to us in a new way. What a wonderful revelation for all God's people who have been following God but have never fully grasped the love of a father and who have never been able to connect with others through love.

The restoration of the Son

When we read the passages of Scriptures that describe Jesus in heaven, we see Him in a new light. God is about to restore the image we have of Jesus.

Revelation 1:13-16 - And in the midst of the seven lampstands One like the Son of Man, clothed with a garment down to the feet and girded about the chest with a golden band. His head and hair were white like wool, as white as snow, and His eyes like a flame of fire; His feet were like fine brass, as if refined in a furnace, and His voice as the sound of many waters; He had in His right hand seven stars, out of His mouth went a sharp two-edged sword, and His countenance was like the sun shining in its strength.

Revelation 19:11-16 - Now I saw heaven opened, and behold, a white horse. And He who sat on him was called Faithful and True, and in righteousness He judges and makes war. His eyes were like a flame of fire, and on His head were many crowns. He had a name written that no one knew except Himself. He was clothed with a robe dipped in blood, and His name is called The Word of God. And the armies in heaven, clothed in fine linen, white and clean, followed Him on white horses. Now out of His mouth goes a sharp sword, that with it He should strike the nations. And He Himself will rule them with a rod of iron. He Himself treads the winepress of the fierceness and wrath of Almighty God. And He has on His robe and on His thigh a name written: King of kings and Lord of lords.

We need to have a revelation of who Jesus really is. Many identify Him as a baby that was born in Bethlehem. Others see Him as a radical prophet who preached about heaven and hell while He was walking on the earth with His followers. Others only have the picture of a Jesus who was beaten, bruised, and hanging on a cross. So many have never advanced further from that image of Him.

God is going to restore the full revelation of who Jesus really is. For example, there are many who believe in Him, but do not believe that He is God. They believe He was a good man, or a prophet sent by God, but not God. Others doubt the miracles that He performed. Others do not believe that He is alive and seated at the right hand of the Father.

Jesus was not just another person who was crucified for His beliefs, but shed the righteous blood of God on the cross and became the spotless Lamb that was sacrificed for all the sins of mankind and when God fully restores the image of His Son, the scales that have blinded people will fall off.

But the restoration of the Son can only come by revelation. Peter walked with Jesus throughout His ministry and witnessed everything He said and did. Yet he did not have a full understanding of who Jesus was until the Holy Spirit revealed Jesus to Him in a new way.

Matthew 16:15-19 - He said to them, "But who do you say that I am?" Simon Peter answered and said, "You are the Christ, the Son of the living God." Jesus answered and said to him, "Blessed are you, Simon Bar-Jonah, for flesh and blood has not revealed this to you, but My Father who is in heaven. And I also say to you that you are Peter, and on this rock I will build My church, and the gates of Hades shall not prevail against it. And I will give you the keys of the kingdom of heaven, and whatever you bind on earth will be bound in heaven, and whatever you loose on earth will be loosed in heaven."

It is only when the fullness of the Son is revealed that we will be able to come together as a powerful church and prevail against the armies of hell and set people free. That is why Paul was convinced that Jesus was God the Son because He saw Him in His rightful place in heaven. He never saw Jesus while He walked on the earth.

John was on the isle of Patmos and God showed him a revelation of what will happen in the last days. He saw all the havoc that the devil is going to cause through political leaders on the earth. It seems that there will be no hope for mankind, but in the midst of all the chaos, John saw Jesus in heaven with all His power and authority who will prevail against the dragon, the beast, and the antichrist and cast them into the lake of fire.

The end times is not about the devil but about Jesus who has full authority over heaven, earth, and hell. He presides over a Kingdom that prevails against its enemies. Kingdoms will come and go, but God's Kingdom is the only kingdom that will last forever and ever.

The coming tribulation is not about the power of the devil, but about the power of God. It does not exalt the kingdom of darkness, but firmly established God's Kingdom. We should be encouraged knowing that Jesus is not trying to destroy us but is fighting for us.

The restoration of gospel

Mark 9:36-38 - Then He took a little child and set him in the midst of them. And when He had taken him in His arms, He said to them, "Whoever receives one of these little children in My name receives Me; and whoever receives Me, receives not Me but Him who sent Me." Now John answered Him, saying, "Teacher, we saw someone who does not follow us casting out demons in Your name, and we forbade him because he does not follow us."

God is preparing us for a worldwide harvest of souls that are ready to hear the gospel. The gospel is the power of heaven that saves nations.

Revelation 14:15 - And another angel came out of the temple, crying with a loud voice to Him who sat on the cloud, "Thrust in Your sickle and reap, for the time has come for You to reap, for the harvest of the earth is ripe."

Matthew 24:14 - And this gospel of the kingdom will be preached in all the world as a witness to all the nations, and then the end will come.

This is a prophetic word for the church today. The gospel is the last sign that has to be fulfilled in the last days. The glory is coming upon the church and the gospel will be preached to every nation. The gospel is about to be restored.

We have a lot of work to do in order to fulfill God's end time plan.

The restoration of the gifts

The ministry of power is going to be restored. The nine gifts of the Spirit are going to operate in power in the last days.

The nine manifestation gifts of the Spirit are listed as follows:

1. Tongues
2. Interpretation of Tongues
3. Gift of Prophecy
4. Word of Knowledge
5. Word of Wisdom
6. Discerning of Spirits
7. Faith
8. Healings
9. Working of Miracles

These gifts belong to the church and are supernatural manifestations of the Holy Spirit and are manifest through Spirit-filled believers. These manifestations are visible expressions of the Holy Spirit and reveal His power. The purpose of the gifts is to equip the church in order to demonstrate the reality of God to unbelievers.

These gifts were given at Pentecost and were used powerfully by the early church. This power has somehow diminished in the church today and before the church can be equipped, the gifts will have to be restored.

If the spirit of Elijah is coming and all things will be restored, we need to look at what Elijah did.

1 Kings 17:1 - And Elijah the Tishbite, of the inhabitants of Gilead, said to Ahab, "As the Lord God of Israel lives, before whom I stand, there shall not be dew nor rain these years, except at my word."

Elijah was a lone voice to the nations in his generation and he confronted kings. The power of the Spirit flowed powerfully through him and he called fire from heaven. It was this power working through Elijah that put to shame the futile efforts of the false prophets who opposed him.

The manifestation of God's power through His Spirit will convince people. God is going to place us before wicked kings and political leaders who are keeping their people in chains. They are going to be confronted and challenged and their inferior power is going to be exposed which will cause the people to turn to God.

We are going to stand fearlessly before rulers on the earth with great boldness and they will have to loose the bondages of religion, tradition, poverty, and slavery from the people because they will not be able to hold them any longer.

The restoration of worship

John 4:23 - But the hour is coming, and now is, when the true worshipers will worship the Father in spirit and truth; for the Father is seeking such to worship Him.

The time is now for worship to be restored. When true worship is released, the many benefits of the Holy Spirit will bring supernatural change to the people of God:

- The water of the Holy Spirit will bring things to life
- The fire of the Holy Spirit will burn up everything that is not of God
- The wind of the Holy Spirit will take the gospel to the ends of the earth
- The wine of the Holy Spirit will cause God's children to walk in the Spirit. They will change and become new wineskins and they will readily receive the new wine

The restoration of the Kingdom

Acts 1:6 - Therefore, when they had come together, they asked Him, saying, "Lord, will You at this time restore the kingdom to Israel?"

Satan's kingdom is about to be pushed back and brought to nothing. God is about to restore His Kingdom on the earth and His full authority and power will be exercised which will crush the enemy once and for all.

God loves those who are created in His image and He is about to take full vengeance on the kingdom of darkness that has destroyed and hurt people and nations for generations. Jesus came to give life to people and the full manifestation and benefits of His Kingdom is about to be restored on the earth.

Isaiah 60:1 - Arise, shine; For your light has come! And the glory of the LORD is risen upon you.

When God's Kingdom is fully restored, there will be no more darkness to dim or block out the light. There will be no need for the sun or the moon to give light to the earth, because Jesus is the light of the world and there will be no more darkness.

1 John 1:5 - This is the message which we have heard from Him and declare to you, that God is light and in Him is no darkness at all.

The restoration of possessions

There are things that have been stolen from us and when God restores all things, He will restore the things that have been taken from us illegally. The devil has stolen our money, our joy, our families, our future, and so much more.

Proverbs 13:22 - A good man leaves an inheritance to his children's children, But the wealth of the sinner is stored up for the righteous.

God is going to restore our dignity, our finances, our families, and our possessions.

The restoration of position

Promotion is coming and our true position with Christ is going to be restored.

So many anointed children of God have been tricked and deceived and have lost their positions, ministries, and reputations. God is going to restore us and will release a fresh anointing upon our lives. We will once again take up our position of authority and take our rightful place with Him as priests and kings.

There is so much more

Revelation 20:6 - Blessed and holy is he who has part in the first resurrection. Over such the second death has no power, but they shall be priests of God and of Christ, and shall reign with Him a thousand years.

The first restoration prepares us to reign with Christ on the earth for 1000 years. After that, the next restoration will follow and we will be part of the new heaven and earth and we will rule and reign together with Him forever and ever. Think about this. We will be with Him when He creates the new heavens and the new earth. What a wonderful privilege. AMEN!

Chapter 5

The Doctrine Of The Kingdom

Not every church represents the true church. That is very clear when we read about the different churches Jesus speaks about in Revelation and His pronouncements on each. The same applies today especially in these final days of the church age.

From Scripture we know that there are going to be two kinds of churches in the last days. They will either be alive or dead.

The true church is apostolic in nature and represents exactly what Christ intends for His bride. It is a church that is equipped, united, and mature and looks like Christ. The apostolic church is what the true church should look like. Not every Christian leader represents the truth of Christ and not every church is the true church. In the same way, the Bible speaks about two doctrines; the apostles' doctrine and the doctrine of demons.

Acts 2:42 - And they continued steadfastly in the apostles' doctrine and fellowship, in the breaking of bread, and in prayers.

Doctrine has become such a bad word in Christian circles because of the controversy it can cause. The church needs to once again go back to the doctrine of the early church in order to test the foundations of their beliefs and that may mean going back to the basics like the doctrine of salvation, the baptism in the Holy spirit, holiness, etc.

The church needs to go back to where it was birthed at Pentecost. We need to go back and see what the early apostles did, what they believed in, what they taught, and what they embraced.

We know that those who were filled with the Holy Spirit continued in the apostles' doctrine after Pentecost which would make us believe that the early apostles set certain standards of beliefs that everyone had to follow.

If we can formulate an understanding of what the apostles' doctrine means, we will have a better understanding of the true doctrine we should follow so that we can prepare for the future.

1. The apostles' doctrine is the truth

The truth will always reflect who Jesus is because He is the truth. False teachings are exposed because they deviate from Jesus. Doctrine can be categorized in two ways; it is either the truth or it is not the truth. There can be no middle ground. The apostles doctrine is the truth.

Mark 1:27 - Then they were all amazed, so that they questioned among themselves, saying, "What is this? What new doctrine is this? For with authority He commands even the unclean spirits, and they obey Him."

Jesus preached the truth and His teaching clashed with the teachings of the Jewish leaders in His day.

The apostles' doctrine does not come from man but from God and comprises of all the principles and laws of heaven that Jesus taught when He preached the gospel of the Kingdom. It reveals the true nature, character, and heart of God. He loves people and wants them to be part of His family. That is why He sent His only Son to pay the price for each and every person on earth and offers eternal life to all those who accept His offer of salvation.

When the Word tells us that they "continued in the apostles' doctrine" it means that they continued in the doctrine of truth. They took what God said and did not change or corrupt His Word. They did not add their own opinions, but rather applied everything that they had learned.

The apostle's doctrine means obeying and applying what God says and not what man says. Man's doctrines are false doctrines, but the doctrine of heaven is the truth and sets people free. Any other doctrine places heavy yokes and burdens onto people.

John 7:16 - Jesus answered them and said, "My doctrine is not Mine, but His who sent Me.

The doctrine of the apostles reflect accurately what God says in His Word.

2 Timothy 4:3-4 - For the time will come when they will not endure sound doctrine, but according to their own desires, because they have itching ears, they will heap up for themselves teachers; and they will turn their ears away from the truth, and be turned aside to fables.

Anything that God has not said in His Word is an alternative way that is not sanctioned by God. But there are those who do not want to obey the truth and find false teachers who will tell them what they want to hear.

2. The apostles' doctrine applies to the church

For the church to fulfill its apostolic mandate in this present season, it has to apply the apostles' doctrine and because it is the doctrine of truth, the church should embrace it and follow it. Jesus is coming for a church that is truly apostolic. If we want to be part of God's end time plan, we must understand the importance of the local church and God's plan for it.

So many people think they are Christians because they believe in Jesus. Well, that is not true because even the demons believe. A true Christian is one who believes in the church of Jesus Christ. Although we need to be committed to Christ, we also need to be committed to the body of Christ. You cannot be committed to Christ unless you are committed to His church. That is the way that Jesus wants it and that is what the apostles' doctrine embraces.

We need to be committed to Christ's bride and love the church as much as Jesus loved the church. Jesus gave His life for the church and we should also be prepared to give our lives for the church.

There are Godly leaders that God has anointed to lead His church, but they will not be able to lead if God's children are not part of the church.

Ephesians 5:32 - This is a great mystery, but I speak concerning Christ and the church.

The church is referred to as the "great mystery" which means that we are joined in one flesh with Christ. The mystery is when men and women come together in harmony and unity that initiates a flow of the anointing oil of the Holy Spirit which brings healing, salvation, and prosperity from heaven to earth.

To be truly apostolic we need to be committed and submitted to Christ's bride. The apostles' doctrine implies that they also continued in fellowship with others. They did not isolate themselves, but reached out to others in love and compassion with an emphasis on gathering together to glorify God.

3. The apostles' doctrine means taking swift action

Acts 2:39-41 - For the promise is to you and to your children, and to all who are afar off, as many as the Lord our God will call." And with many other words he testified and exhorted them, saying, "Be saved from this perverse generation." Then those who gladly received his word were baptized; and that day about three thousand souls were added to them.

Immediately after receiving the power of God's Spirit, the apostles organized themselves to reach others who needed to be saved.

A lot of people come to church Sunday after Sunday hoping that the pastor or some leader will recognize their gift. But you do not need anyone's permission to exercise your gift. You can go to hospitals and old age homes at any time. They are eagerly awaiting your gift!

There are so many people who are lonely and need encouragement. God does not want you to sit around waiting for someone to promote you into ministry. You can lay hands on sick people. You will be surprised how many sick people are out there crying out for someone who cares and who is willing to pray for them. Jesus never waited. The power of God's Spirit came upon Him at the Jordan River and after a time of temptation, He started His ministry.

He entered the streets of the city and found multitudes of desperate people who needed prayer. But He never isolated Himself from His disciples. He fellowshipped regularly with those who followed Him. That is an apostolic attitude that is needed today.

The apostle's doctrine means taking quick action. The most powerful pulpit you can have is your desk at the office or your work bench in the factory. God has placed you in the work place so that you can tell people that there is a Jesus that cares.

This promise is for everyone and extends into the future until Jesus returns. God is waiting for those with an apostolic heart to look for people who are hurting and tormented. You are the answer because God has equipped every one of us for the task.

4. The apostle's doctrine releases increase.

Acts 2:47 - Praising God and having favor with all the people. And the Lord added to the church daily those who were being saved.

When you start embracing the truth, God will start blessing you. The Bible teaches us that those who labor in the Word and doctrine are worthy of double honor. A true apostolic church will always grow. People are attracted to the truth. Not every church has to be a mega church, but there must be growth. Churches that reach beyond the walls of their buildings usually increase in abundant blessings of the Lord.

Churches who have a heart for unsaved people will find unsaved people coming to their churches. I always give an altar call because I know that if I do not, God will send the unsaved somewhere else where they can have an opportunity to give their lives to Jesus. I never wait for people who ask to be baptized. I announce water baptismal services and fill the baptismal bath by faith. It has never been in vain.

I always allow people to receive the baptism in the Holy Spirit because doing so fulfills an apostolic responsibility. There is coming a mighty move of God upon the face of the earth and God is going to use His church to reach out to every nation. Now is a good time to practice and to make the apostles' doctrine our doctrine.

There are churches who are going to be involved in God's plan, but there will also be those who will miss the move of God.

5. The apostles' doctrine implies discipleship

Acts 2:42 - And they continued steadfastly in the apostles' doctrine.

What I really love about this passage of the Word is that the writer did not refer to God's doctrine or Jesus' doctrine. God recognizes His earthly leaders who are heading His church. We cannot serve God if we do not serve an earthly leader.

What this passage means is that the people who are leading you and mentoring you have made the doctrine of heaven their own doctrine and this also implies discipleship. God has appointed them because Godly leaders have disciples.

Who are you following? Who is mentoring you? Are you with the right leader? Do not just follow anyone. I teach my people to ask their leaders hard questions before they follow them. There is nothing wrong with that because leaders can either take you to a good place or to a bad place, depending on the principles they apply in their own lives.

Look at the fruit they are producing in their lives as that is what they will produce in your life. For example, are they successful in their marriage and family? Are they blessed financially, or do they live in lack and failure? The apostolic anointing on a leader's life will be in proportion to the measure they reflect Kingdom values and fruit.

You must be able to be inspired by the person you are following and have a desire to excel as much as they have excelled in all things. That way you will know if you are going to walk in an apostolic anointing.

6. The apostle's doctrine means faithfulness

Acts 2:42 - And they continued steadfastly...

In order for the church to be stable, believers need to be faithful. This is sadly lacking in the church today. Most Christians do not want to become involved and prefer to come to church on a Sunday just to listen to the Word and leave again. But if the church is going to become truly apostolic, the people need to become more involved and more stable.

Too many of God's people are wandering aimlessly from one church to the next, or from one conference to the next. God has not called us to be wanderers but is looking for those who know their purpose and know where they should be planted. A commitment to a church should be a long term covenant and could even be a lifetime commitment. I say this with caution, but it is not unthinkable. Children need stability and when parents move from church to church, their children also become unstable.

There are so many anointed men and women who were once on fire for God, but have become lukewarm in their faith and do not even go to church. Many say that they have given up on the church. But Jesus has not given up on the church and that is a good reason to become stable and serve the Lord with other believers. Find a church that has leaders who are stable and allow God to fulfill your spiritual mandate in that place.

7. The apostle's doctrine means fulfilling your purpose

John 7:17 - If anyone wills to do His will, he shall know concerning the doctrine, whether it is from God or whether I speak on My own authority.

Every one of us have been given an assignment to fulfill during our lifetime on earth and it is a divine mandate that comes from heaven. Each one of us have been created for a specific purpose and we can implement the apostles' doctrine by obediently doing what God wants us to do in our lifetime.

Your purpose will always advance God's agenda and not your own agenda. It will definitely not advance a worldly agenda.

Your purpose will have everything to do with building God's Kingdom and not your own kingdom. There are only two kingdoms and anything that does not build His Kingdom benefits Satan's kingdom. Your purpose is to benefit God's Kingdom.

Each one of us are called to fulfill a unique purpose. If you are doing what everybody else is doing, you are probably walking in someone else's destiny because the anointing on your life is a unique anointing. God wants you to be different and to go where nobody else has gone before.

You are wonderfully and beautifully made in God's image and He has written a book about your life even before you were born. I encourage you to pursue God and find out what He has written about you. He will give you a step by step and day by day guide if you fellowship and build a bond with Him. That is the only way to do it.

Separate yourself from the daily hustle and bustle and find a quiet place each and every day where you cannot be interrupted. You will be amazed to see how much God has to say to you! What will God say to you? It will always incorporate what He wants you to do so that you can represent Him and work with Him to build His Kingdom. It is as simple as that. God is not complicated and will never require you to do anything that you are unable to do. Through

His Spirit, you will be able to accomplish the impossible. Just trust Him because He will never shame you or disappoint you.

8. The apostle's doctrine is the Kingdom of God

Mark 1:14 - Now after John was put in prison, Jesus came to Galilee, preaching the gospel of the kingdom of God

Jesus spent most of His time in ministry preaching about the Kingdom of God. He took a lot of time explaining what God's Kingdom was like. He did that so that we can understand how to represent His Kingdom to others.

Each believer is required to be a careful and responsible caretaker of that which has been entrusted to them. It involves activities that glorify God and represents God's Kingdom to all the people on the earth today.

The Kingdom of God is the divine authority and rule given by the Father to the Son. Christ will exercise this rule until He has subdued all that is hostile to God.

The Kingdom of God refers to man's submission to God as the undisputed authority of the church and the practical application of His will. Believers enter the Kingdom of God when they are born again and the Kingdom operates through those He has called, ordained, and anointed.

Every time Jesus sent out ministers to proclaim the Kingdom of God, He sent them out with power. God has given each and every one of us gifts, talents, and callings that should be used for the advancement of His Kingdom and to win over others for Him. During our lifetime on earth, all our time and effort should equate to Kingdom brick and mortar, or else it is a waste of time.

Jesus preached the gospel of the Kingdom to poor people so that they could learn to defeat poverty.

The difference between God's Kingdom and worldly kingdoms is that God's Kingdom is everlasting. Organizations will come and go, but God's Kingdom will remain forever.

Choose to invest your time and talents in God's Kingdom and be a good steward of everything He has entrusted to you. Do not waste your time building the kingdoms of this world. God wants you to have a position in His Kingdom. Do everything as if you are doing it unto the Lord because when you are faithful, God will promote you.

The apostles' doctrine proclaims the Kingdom message of divine healing, signs and wonders, miracles, financial blessings, safety and protection in a dangerous world. That is what Jesus preached. He brought light and hope into a dark world filled with hopelessness.

We cannot separate the teachings of the Lord from the 21st century church. Our apostolic responsibility is to release the same light and hope that Jesus did when He was on earth.

Any church that wants to be apostolic needs to do the works of Jesus and represent God's Kingdom on earth.

Chapter 6

Apostolic Sounds

There were thousands of people who followed Jesus while He was ministering on earth, but only one hundred and twenty caught the move of God. This small group positioned themselves in the right place to receive from God. They were the few who had the heart of God and knew that something was about to come upon the earth.

Today God is looking for those who know what His plan is for this generation and where they need to be in order to receive it. There are certain sounds that come from heaven which are heard by those who are in tune with God and we need to hear what the Spirit is telling us in these unique times.

1 Corinthians 14:7-9 - Even things without life, whether flute or harp, when they make a sound, unless they make a distinction in the sounds, how will it be known what is piped or played? For if the trumpet makes an uncertain sound, who will prepare himself for battle? So likewise you, unless you utter by the tongue words easy to understand, how will it be known what is spoken? For you will be speaking into the air.

God wants His children to hear clearly and distinctly so that they can replicate and interpret the sounds of heaven. What God is saying today is what the church should be saying, but not every believer today is saying what God is saying and not every church is saying what God is saying.

There are certain sounds that the church should be making. Every sound carries a message. These sounds can be heard in the spirit realm, but they do not all necessary come from the Spirit of God. There are sounds that come from the demonic realm, from the human spirit, and sounds that come from heaven.

There are certain sounds that are distinct but there are also uncertain sounds or indistinct sounds. The sounds the church is making today should be distinct, certain, and clear so that God's people can know exactly what they need to do.

But sadly, there are many mixed messages in the church, in the home, and in society which can bring confusion in the body of Christ and God is not a God of confusion. The sounds that we hear from heaven are distinct and clear and should be directing us to our goal as a body of believers.

The military used various sounds with musical instruments that gave certain instructions especially in times of battle. The trumpet would be used which would make certain sounds and each sound represented a command which the troops would respond to. The sound could be heard above the sound of gunfire and explosions. If the trumpeter made an uncertain sound, then the message would be uncertain.

For example, the person blowing the trumpet or bugle would blow "reveille" and every soldier knew it was time to rise and meet in company formation. There was also the sound of "attack" when in battle. When a commander wanted the troops to charge or to attack the enemy, the person blowing the trumpet or bugle would blow the "charge" which told the troops to advance towards the enemy in battle. It had to be a certain distinct sound. There was also the sound of "retreat" which meant lights had to be out and everyone had to go to bed. Just imagine if the trumpeter blew the sound of retreat in the middle of the battle. That would be a disaster!

Sounds in the church

We are living in serious times and it seems that the wrong sounds are being played in the church today. God's people are sleeping instead of standing up in formation ready to do battle. The church today needs to send out the right sounds in the right sequence.

John 3:8 - The wind blows where it wishes, and you hear the sound of it, but cannot tell where it comes from and where it goes. So is everyone who is born of the Spirit.

Christian leaders need to carry a sound and a message to the church that will lead them to the right place. There are apostolic sounds that need to be heard. There are prophetic sounds that need to be uttered. God has given us the sound of victory, salvation, hope, and deliverance.

Each and every born again Spirit-filled believer today, carries the sound of heaven within them. We carry a sound of life and where there is death, we can release the sound of life.

Listen to those who are in the Spirit and you find that they make sounds that are different from the sounds of worldly people. They carry the sounds that reflect the power of God. Sounds of anger, hatred, and bitterness are not sounds that come from heaven. They come from another place. The sounds that God's children make should reflect the sounds of heaven. You will know if somebody is on fire for God because of the sounds they make.

There are distinct sounds that prepare us for God's plans. They are not the sounds of yesterday. They are new sounds that are very distinct and proclaim God's blueprint for the church today. These are the prophetic sounds that reveal the secrets of God and are preparing us for the purpose and mandate of the end time church.

Prophetically, we are living in the end time church which is going to end in victory, but the Laodicean church is making sounds of compromise that reveal its lukewarm attitude to God. There has to be a clear distinction in the sounds the church should be making and the sounds the world is making. We need to survive in the realm and the atmosphere of the Holy Spirit and not in the atmosphere of the world. We are not here to be worldly but rather we are here to be Godly. The church needs to stop making these worldly sounds.

Sounds that come from the spirit realm can come from any one of three sources. They are either demonic, or from our own flesh, or they are from God.

When you hear a sound you are always going to react to it. The sounds that come from a demonic source will always deceive you and it will cause oppression and depression. Sounds that come from the flesh will cause you to be tempted with fleshly desires which lead to sin. Sounds that come from God will always bring joy, hope, and peace.

Voices that come from heaven will always lead you to do what is right. It will always encourage, comfort, and exalt you. It will convict you of sin.

God's children should replicate the sounds from heaven so that others can be blessed, healed, and delivered.

Today the church should be hearing distinct sounds from heaven urging believers to prepare for revival. Like the voice of John the Baptist who cried out, "The Kingdom of Heaven is at hand. Repent. Prepare the way of the Lord." The sounds he was making was for his generation and they were clear distinct sounds which made a way for Jesus to release the anointing.

These same sounds are once again being proclaimed prophetically but not everyone is listening. But those who are hearing the sounds, are preparing for it. They are waiting for it and are expecting it. God is going to surprise many in the last days. He did it when He arrived on earth as a baby born in Bethlehem.

What sounds are you making? Are they distinct and clear? The sounds that you make are the sounds that others will hear. What sounds are you hearing? Have you noticed that a child will always try to replicate the sounds that they hear because that is how they learn to speak? The more you spend time with your Father in heaven, the more you are going to hear sounds from heaven which means you are going to be speaking and replicating the sounds that God is making.

Apostolic sounds

Numbers 23:21 - The Lord his God is with him, and the shout of a king is among them.

God has always used the voice of His true leaders to prepare His children. They have made certain distinct sounds which have been heard by the people and caused them to make preparation.

Each member of the five-fold ministry carries a sound that releases a particular anointing and prepares and equips God's children for His plan.

- The voice of the pastor - encourages, leads, and admonishes the sheep
- The voice of the prophet - sees the future and speaks to the church in order to prepare them for what is coming
- The voice of the teacher - instructs and trains the church in the Word
- The voice of the evangelist - preaches the message of salvation to the lost
- The voice of the apostle - leads the church in accordance with God' s plan for a particular season and generation

In the present time, the church has been hearing the sounds made by pastors, teachers, evangelist, prophets. But we have not heard the sounds of the apostle. God is restoring the voice of the apostle to the church which will cause all five ministry gifts to be released and they will all speak with one voice which will call God's people to a place where they can be equipped and sent out with great authority and power. They will be distinct and clear sounds which will activate the church for its final mandate on earth.

Romans 10:18 - But I say, have they not heard? Yes indeed: "Their sounds has gone out to all the earth, and their words to the ends of the world."

Chapter 7

The Glory Of The Church

Most Christians today believe that there is a coming move of God, but we do not really know how it is going to manifest itself or how the church is going to react to it.

Revival has always been about God's people and is received by those who are seeking it. It will never come upon those who are not looking for it. If one studies all the revivals throughout church history, we discover that revival only came when men and women united together and started seeking God through prayer and fasting.

The first revival of the church was poured out on the one hundred and twenty in the Upper Room at Pentecost. They gathered together in unity and started praying. They believed Jesus when He told them that the outpouring of God's Spirit would come upon them and they did not stop believing until they received the Promise of the Holy Spirit.

We need to have an expectation of the coming revival upon the church that will empower us to take the gospel of Jesus to every nation in these last days. We need to know that heaven is about to break out upon the earth.

Joel 2:28-29 - And it shall come to pass afterward That I will pour out My Spirit on all flesh; Your sons and your daughters shall prophesy, Your old men shall dream dreams, Your young men shall see visions. And also on My menservants and on My maidservants I will pour out My Spirit in those days.

Joel prophesied that God would pour out His Spirit upon everyone and this happened on the Day of Pentecost which marked the beginning of the church age. The purpose of this outpouring at Pentecost was to empower men and women of God to minister to others and to overcome the power of the enemy. God has empowered each Spirit-filled believer to rescue someone out of the clutches of the devil.

1 Peter 5:8 - Be sober, be vigilant; because your adversary the devil walks about like a roaring lion, seeking whom he may devour.

In the Old Testament the Holy Spirit only came upon priests, kings, prophets, and special individuals who were anointed for a special task. We are God's special people in these days and through the anointing we can function in our unique ability.

Pentecost marks the official beginning of the church and the era of the Holy Spirit upon all believers. Over the past 2000 years from the birth of the church age, there have been many revivals and they have always been similar to what happened at Pentecost. Most notably was the Azusa Street revival in Los Angeles in the early 1900's. God's power and Spirit came upon a small gathering of believers and once again the gifts and power of the Holy Spirit was given to the church through tongues and other manifestations. For about 1900 years, there was very little evidence that the church functioned in the full power of Pentecost. God restored that which was lost for so many centuries and He is once again about to do something that will transform the church entirely.

Peter prophesied that there will be a revival in the last days which will affect the entire world.

We are taught that the benefits of the New Covenant are better than the Old Covenant yet there were many mighty manifestations of God's Spirit experienced by His people in the Old Testament that were greater than those experienced in the New Testament church. There were manifestations that we have not yet experienced. However we are about to see manifestations of God's glory that has never been experienced by the church before.

On the Day of Pentecost, the Holy Spirit was poured out on all flesh. Men and women, Jews and Gentiles, rich and poor, free and slave, young and old, were all baptized in the Holy Spirit. God never sends anyone on a divine mission unless He has anointed them first.

Perhaps this may sound a bit controversial, but there will not be another outpouring of God's Spirit in this last move of God. Jesus sent the Holy Spirit 2000 years ago and all Spirit-filled believers are already anointed for ministry.

The glory of the Father

Just as the Holy Spirit comes from Jesus, the glory comes from the Father. That is the Father's outpouring that will be released upon the church soon. The glory of God relates to the heart of the Father, His love, and all His attributes.

We have responsibilities

Children born in royal families are taught that they have responsibilities and duties to perform and they are trained and disciplined from birth. They grow up under constant supervision and mentorship because they represent the Crown.

Sadly, believers today do not understand their royal position in terms of conduct, duty, and responsibility. They do not believe it is necessary for them to learn, grow, or submit because they mistakenly believe that they can live any way they want to because they are "King's kids." That is not how it works in worldly kingdoms and it certainly should not be the case in God's Kingdom's. Each and every member of God's royal family has a place and purpose which has to be carried out in a responsible way.

We represent the King of kings and it is our Kingdom responsibility to do everything in our power to learn how we can best represent the King. That means we have to fulfill our duties in the Kingdom as we advance the King's agenda.

1 Peter 2:9 - But you are a chosen generation, a royal priesthood, a holy nation, His own special people, that you may proclaim the praises of Him who called you out of darkness into His marvelous light.

The church needs to be transformed and function fully in its royal mandate so that God's children can be respected as members of the Royal household. It will be the glory of God upon the church that will reflect the glory of the King so that it can draw others to it. Only then will the church really represent God and the things that are in heaven. (Glory denotes great honor and distinction and is a high, praiseworthy asset, adoration, majestic beauty, and splendor.) The glory of God will take us from a weak position to a strong position and others in the world will know that we reflect who Christ is. This is a place where the church has never been before. God's glory will be poured out onto the church in the coming days which will make us relevant to the world. It is the glory of God that will give us favor to stand before kings and represent the authority of heaven.

The glory of God means heaven touching earth. The anointing empowers us but the glory on us, reflects the power and beauty of heaven and when Jesus sees us, He will see Himself. When the enemy sees us, he will see Christ and he will have no more fight left in him.

The anointing of the Holy Spirit empowers you to defeat the enemy, but the glory of God shows others who you represent. The anointing enables you to minister to others, but the glory enables you to enjoy full Kingdom benefits. The anointing is the power of God's Spirit, but the glory is the beauty of His Spirit.

We must admit that the church is certainly not enjoying Kingdom benefits. But the benefits will come with the glory. God's people will represent heaven on earth.

There have been many moves and manifestations of the Spirit in the past, but the best is yet to come. What the church has experienced in the past is only a type and shadow of the glory that is coming. There are much better things coming than a bit of laughter and gold dust on your forehead. God allowed some of that for a short while, but there are greater things coming with a greater testimony and lasting fruit. People in the world will no longer mock us or laugh at us. Those days are coming to an end. The glory of God upon your life will not be explained away by confused theologians. Everyone will know it is God's true manifestation.

Haggai 2:9 - 'The glory of this latter temple shall be greater than the former,' says the Lord of hosts. 'And in this place I will give peace,' says the Lord of hosts."

The past glory

In order to have an expectation and faith for the coming glory, we need to first look at the glory of God in the Old Testament.

Exodus 16:10 - Now it came to pass, as Aaron spoke to the whole congregation of the children of Israel, that they looked toward the wilderness, and behold, the glory of the Lord appeared in the cloud.

Everyone saw the glory of God. They saw the glory with their physical eyes. It was experienced by the Israelites thousands of years ago and it is going to happen to the church even in a greater way. It has not happened yet but it is going to happen.

Exodus 24:16 - And the glory of the Lord stayed on Mount Sinai, and the cloud covered it six days: and the seventh day he called to Moses out of the middle of the cloud.

Exodus 40:34-35 - Then the cloud covered the tabernacle of meeting, and the glory of the Lord filled the tabernacle. And Moses was not able to enter the tabernacle of meeting, because the cloud rested above it, and the glory of the Lord filled the tabernacle.

The glory of the church

If we translate this to the present time, it means the glory of God is going to enter our church buildings and rest above it. That is the least we can expect to happen. That is what happened in the Old Testament and it is going to happen in the church. This prophecy is still to be fulfilled.

We have been expecting an outpouring of the Spirit, but that has already come at Pentecost. We have all the power we need. We do not need any more. What we need is the glory of God. That is what is going to separate us in these last days. That is what is going to make the church the true church and that is what will expose the false church. They are either going to be under the cloud or there is going to be no cloud.

> *1 Kings 8:10-11 - And it came to pass, when the priests came out of the holy place, that the cloud filled the house of the Lord, so that the priests could not continue ministering because of the cloud; for the glory of the Lord filled the house of the Lord.*

God must be given all the glory instead of man taking all the glory. The glory of God will fill His house and silence the voice of man so that the people can listen to God.

With every revival, there has always been a charismatic superstar-like hero. Today, many church leaders are worshipped like Hollywood stars. Men and women have the tendency to hijack God's revival with their charismatic ability and woo the crowds. That has been the characteristics of past revivals with all the fleshly outcomes, but only God is going to receive the glory in the coming revival. The people will not be looking at man because their eyes will be transfixed on the glory. It is time that God is given glory and not people or buildings.

Judgment must begin in the house of God and this is not to punish the people, but to encourage them to submit to God. We should willingly lie down and worship the God of glory.

The true anointed vessels of God will rise up from the floor in the midst of the glory and begin to bring the body of believers to perfection and a mighty army will rise up under the command of the apostles who will transform nations with their testimony.

Jesus experienced the glory

Mark 9:2-3 - Now after six days Jesus took Peter, James, and John, and led them up on a high mountain apart by themselves; and He was transfigured before them. His clothes became shining, exceedingly white, like snow, such as no launderer on earth can whiten them.

Jesus experienced God's glory which was seen by Peter, James, and John.

Mark 9:5-7 - Then Peter answered and said to Jesus, "Rabbi, it is good for us to be here; and let us make three tabernacles: one for You, one for Moses, and one for Elijah"- because he did not know what to say, for they were greatly afraid. And a cloud came and overshadowed them; and a voice came out of the cloud, saying, "This is My beloved Son. Hear Him!"

Although it seemed that Peter did not know what to say, he actually made a powerful prophetic utterance. Prophetically, he said "Come on let us build churches, so that this glory can come into the churches." In his ignorance, he was prophesying right into the church age because he said, "This glory is going to come into the church and it is going to glorify Jesus."

When the glory came upon Moses, his face shone and everyone saw the glory. They had to put a veil over his face because it was so bright. I believe this is going to be a means of identifying the true believers.

2 Corinthians 3:18 - But we all, with unveiled face, beholding as in a mirror the glory of the Lord, are being transformed into the same image from glory to glory, just as by the Spirit of the Lord.

The faces of God's children are going to shine but they will not put on a veil to hide the glory because it will identify them as God's true representatives on the earth.

Haggai 2:9 - 'The glory of this latter temple shall be greater than the former,' says the Lord of hosts. 'And in this place I will give peace,' says the Lord of hosts."

The glory that is coming into the church in the 21st century is going to be greater than the glory that has been seen in the past. It will release a mighty revival and the gospel will be preached to every nation before the end comes.

Habakkuk 2:14 - For the earth shall be filled with the knowledge of the glory of the Lord, as the waters cover the sea.

How will the entire world be filled with the glory of the Lord? We are going to be carriers of the glory of God together with the Word. The church will go into dangerous places to rescue millions from hell. The glory of God is going to spread right across the earth in the last days. This is greatest time to be alive on the earth. Even in the midst of all the storms that are gathering on the horizon, we will not be moved. The world is about to experience unprecedented financial problems, natural disasters, global conflicts, incurable diseases, and sorrows, but those who carry the glory will be bearers of the good news. God is not angry with people. He plan is to deal with Satan who has deceived the nations. Everyone on earth will be given an opportunity to accept Jesus.

God is about to do something great upon the earth. It is going to happen soon and He is going to use us. The world has nothing to offer anyone but Jesus has everything to offer. He is our hope and our future.

A new song

In every revival in history, new songs have been written that identify with that particular move of God.

Revelation 15:3 - And they sing the song of Moses the servant of God, and the song of the Lamb, saying, great and marvelous are your works, Lord God Almighty; just and true are your ways, you King of saints.

We are going to sing a new song in this revival. I call it the "Revelation 15:3 song of

Moses", because Moses was the initiator of the glory of God. Thank God for the pioneers. Moses persevered. He was severely tormented by the people, but he took all the instructions he received from God in the cloud and made the people do what God wanted. He taught them all the principles of life and death.

New songs should be written in anticipation of this prophetic picture of the church. Are you ready for the glory of God?

Chapter 8

The Twelve Apostolic Types

Throughout history God has always used people to build His Kingdom and He has always raised up the right leaders for each generation to fulfill His purposes for that particular season. These leaders represented God and were sent by Him to advance His plans. Depending on the mission, God would send a person who had the unique characteristics needed to perform the task. They functioned in an apostolic anointing that empowered them to overcome any obstacles placed by the enemy to hinder God's work which generally involved the nations.

After Pentecost, the apostolic ministry was birthed and the apostles were sent by God to preach the gospel everywhere and to establish churches. But these were men and women who were anointed by God to establish His purposes for that time and season.

Therefore, the apostles were no different to those who were sent by God in previous generations to represent and fulfill God's plan. All these leaders functioned in an apostolic anointing and carried out specific tasks which God wanted performed.

This defines the apostolic anointing more broadly and accurately which expands the role of the apostle from creation to the present-day church. Although the word "apostle" was only used in the New Testament after Pentecost, this anointing has always been evident and is more clearly understood when we look at how great men and women were used apostolically in the Old and New Testaments.

This sets a good foundation for their intended role in the end time plan of God which incorporates the church and helps us to better prepare ourselves for God's strategies in this season.

History teaches us that those who were used by God apostolically generally completed what God called them to do by fulfilling their apostolic mandate which added to the expansion of God's Kingdom.

When we study the life of the people who God used in both the Old and New Testaments, we find that most of them functioned in an apostolic anointing in order to fulfill God's plan for the nations and the earth.

I have included the twelve main types which shows us how God used people to bring about His purposes on the earth. I have included men and women that were used apostolically by God in both the Old and New Testaments.

1. The apostolic fulfillment of Noah

(Apostolic mandate: a voice to the nations)

Genesis 6:13-15 - And God said to Noah, "The end of all flesh has come before Me, for the earth is filled with violence through them; and behold, I will destroy them with the earth. "Make yourself an ark of gopherwood; make rooms in the ark, and cover it inside and outside with pitch. "And this is how you shall make it: The length of the ark shall be three hundred cubits, its width fifty cubits, and its height thirty cubits."

Noah was an apostolic voice to the nations exhorting them to turn away from their violence and corrupt lifestyles so that they could be saved. God's plan was to save those who made a choice to turn away from their wickedness and He gave Noah the blueprint for the ark.

Sadly, only his family heeded this apostolic warning and only eight people entered the ark. All those who had rejected the message were destroyed in the flood. This was a sad moment in the history of the nations because many of the people were very familiar with the story of creation and the fall of Adam and Eve. They had first-hand accounts of Eden because many of these people lived up to nine hundred years of age.

But yet they chose to rebel against God and to reject His love and salvation and were destroyed by the flood.

Matthew 24:37-42 - But as the days of Noah were, so also will the coming of the Son of Man be. For as in the days before the flood, they were

> *eating and drinking, marrying and giving in marriage, until the day that Noah entered the ark, and did not know until the flood came and took them all away, so also will the coming of the Son of Man be. Then two men will be in the field: one will be taken and the other left. Two women will be grinding at the mill: one will be taken and the other left. Watch therefore, for you do not know what hour your Lord is coming.*

The Bible tells us that this same spirit of rebellion will prevail in the last days. God is raising up apostolic voices today warning of the coming destruction. In the midst of great wickedness and sin, God is about to raise up His apostles who will take the message of love, hope, and salvation to the nations in the last days. History has a way of repeating itself and we will see many millions and millions of people from all nations who will be destroyed in the coming tribulation.

But God is merciful and will send out His children with the apostolic mantle of Noah who will proclaim the message of salvation.

There is coming a shaking in these last days.

Joel 3:16 - The Lord also will roar from Zion, And utter His voice from Jerusalem; The heavens and earth will shake; But the LORD will be a shelter for His people, And the strength of the children of Israel.

Many people wonder why God is going to shake heaven. When God shakes things, there are things that stand and things that fall and when God shakes heaven, Satan is going to fall from heaven where he walks in and out to accuse us before God. He is going to be cast out onto the earth and prohibited from ever entering into God's presence again. He is going to be very angry and will cause great sorrow and tribulation on the earth.

Luke - 10:18 - And He said to them, "I saw Satan fall like lightning from heaven.

But God is in control. He has always empowered His chosen vessels with an apostolic anointing to perform His will and to advance His agenda. Although it may seem that the devil is in control, only God controls everything in heaven, on the earth, and under the earth. God's plan and His children will always prevail!

2. The apostolic fulfillment of Abraham

(Apostolic mandate: birth a nation.)

Abraham came from a very rich family and was very successful and did not have to seek any opportunities away from his country.

But God had greater plans for him and one day God told him to move to another country. In those days, just travelling over the nearest mountain range was a journey into the unknown with certain dangers. He could so easily have resisted God and remained in his comfort zone.

But Abraham trusted God and believed by faith that he had a greater purpose and destiny to fulfill and he was willing to take the risk in order to discover what God had for him.

Abraham took his wife, his family, his servants, his livestock, and his other possessions and began a journey of faith. He did not know where he was going to but he trusted God for the unknown.

From that day onward, God blessed him much more than he had ever been blessed because of his obedience and faith.

Nations were blessed and protected through Abraham and a new nation was born supernaturally from his seed. The Bible tells us that Sarah gave birth to Isaac at around ninety years of age which was way past her natural ability to conceive, and a new nation was born through Abraham's grandson Israel.

This is how God challenges us. If Abraham had not taken the risk and followed God, he would not have fulfilled his divine calling. His obedience affected every generation even up to the present time. We have no idea to what extent God wants to use us and when we are obedient, our descendants benefit from our faith.

God's promises cannot be processed in the natural mind and you can just imagine how many sincere men and women of God have missed God's plan because they wanted to understand God's calling. If you can work it out in your natural mind, it is probably not God. Many times, God works with those things that do not make any sense at all. They are not logical, they cannot be seen, and they cannot be summed up. They only manifest their greatness after the journey is taken by faith without any natural milestones along the way.

God's people tend to want everything packaged nice and tidily with a GPS, a map, provisions, and a clearly defined destination. Well, God does not work that way. We either trust Him regardless, or we can stay where we are and achieve nothing for His Kingdom.

The things of God always move us somewhere. They can move us spiritually, take us to new levels and heights with Him, or they can move us geographically. Whatever it is, we must always cooperate with the challenges God gives us and when He speaks, we must move.

God's ways are not our ways. When you read the story of Abraham, one can easily conclude that he had fulfilled his Godly destiny after his wife Sarah died when he was one hundred and twenty seven years of age. But that was not the case. Abraham remarried and God allowed him to enjoy another season of his life. God gave him more children and he went on to live another forty years or so and died at the age of one hundred and seventy five years of age.

Because of his faith in God, Abraham enjoyed a long life and was blessed by God. There is so much more to your life than what you are seeing right now. Are you willing to believe God as Abraham did? Surely we can say Abraham fulfilled his apostolic mandate.

Do not ever give up on God. Fulfill your destiny. It does not matter where you are today or how desperate and impossible your situation looks. God is trying to get your attention and is looking for ways to bless you so that you and your family can do the unthinkable in the name of Jesus.

• • •

Remember, while you are alive, God can do things in your life that exceeds what He did in anyone else's life. Abraham's obituary has been written because he has lived and died. But you are still alive and that means the final chapter has not been written. Do not wait until it is too late.

Abraham fulfilled his apostolic mandate by believing God and establishing the Jewish nation.

3. The apostolic fulfillment of Joseph

(Apostolic mandate: save Israel.)

Joseph was thrown into an Egyptian prison at a very young age and to this young boy of seventeen, it must have seemed to him that he did not have a future. Can you imagine how he must have felt each and every day when he woke up. There could not have been much to encourage him and he could so easily have sunk into despair and hopelessness.

I am sure there are so many of God's children who feel this way about their life as they consider their personal circumstances, whether it is their business, marriage, family, or anything else in their life that seems to have no future.

Do not ever give up on God, because He can turn your circumstances around in one day. Joseph never gave up on God. I can just imagine how he would have meditated on the things his father had taught him about God while he was growing up and it was probably those thoughts that encouraged and caused him to trust in God and continue to cultivate a relationship with Him.

Genesis 41:38-41 - And Pharaoh said to his servants, "Can we find such a one as this, a man in whom is the Spirit of God?" Then Pharaoh said to Joseph, "Inasmuch as God has shown you all this, there is no one as discerning and wise as you. You shall be over my house, and all my people shall be ruled according to your word; only in regard to the throne will I be greater than you." And Pharaoh said to Joseph, "See, I have set you over all the land of Egypt."

There came a day when God gave Pharaoh a dream which he wanted interpreted and the only person who could do that for him, was a young Hebrew boy who was serving a life sentence in Pharaoh's jail. From that day onward, Joseph was released from prison and was promoted instantly from prisoner to Prime Minister!

Joseph fulfilled his apostolic mandate by saving Israel from famine and hunger which could have destroyed the entire nation and God's plan for His people.

4. The apostolic fulfillment of Moses

(Apostolic mandate: instruct the nation in the Word.)

Moses had a burning desire to see God's glory. When he went up the mountain, he lingered in God's presence for forty days and forty nights. He stayed in that heavenly environment and when he came down from the mountain, he brought a part of heaven with him which is with us even today.

From the day Moses encountered God at the burning bush, he embarked on a journey with God that he never anticipated. As he implemented God's plan, he preserved the entire nation of Israel who eventually went into the Promised Land and received their inheritance.

Because Moses desired more of God's presence, he took back with him the Word of God which is the foundation of every born-again believer today. When you place a demand on God for the fulfillment of your life, it not only touches you, but touches nations and future generations.

Moses had a great struggle with the task God had given him. He had great opposition from Pharaoh which seemed unending because no matter what God sent by way of destruction to Egypt, Pharaoh would not relent. It took the death of all the firstborn aligned to Pharaohs kingdom to eventually persuade him and he reluctantly allowed the Israelites to leave Egypt.

But after they had left, he changed his mind and pursued God's people. It took the miracle of the Red Sea to stop his campaign of relentless harassment against the Israelites.

After that, Moses had to deal with a constant barrage of rebellion against him and God by his own people. This eventually caused God to delay their entry into the Promised Land for forty years. A promise that should have taken days took decades to be realized. In addition,

Moses was not allowed to enter into the Promised Land.

We must realize that some assignments that God gives us can stretch us to our limits. We see the apostle Paul struggle with the same opposition in his apostolic pursuit to take the Kingdom message to the nations.

But God allowed Moses a greater entrance into His presence and gave him the Law and the pattern for the tabernacle. The apostolic anointing brought him face to face with God and he witnessed the glory of God as he entered the secret place with the Most High God.

5. The apostolic fulfillment of Joshua

(Apostolic mandate: give the nation their inheritance.)

After Moses died, God anointed Joshua to take the Israelites into the Promised Land.

Joshua 4:14 - On that day the Lord magnified Joshua in the sight of all Israel; and they feared him, as they had feared Moses, all the days of his life.

It was a great task because the inhabitants had to be forcefully removed and the land given to each of the twelve tribes as an inheritance. Joshua met the Lord personally which gave him great courage and boldness to take on this great task. This is a characteristic of the apostolic anointing.

Joshua 5:14 - So He said, "No, but as Commander of the army of the LORD I have now come." And Joshua fell on his face to the earth and worshiped, and said to Him, "What does my Lord say to His servant?"

The anointing on our lives will ensure the defeat of our enemy. The apostolic anointing will empower God's people to break the yokes and bondages off the nations in Jesus name.

Joshua exerted great apostolic power when he spoke to the sun and moon and they obeyed him. That has never been repeated in any other generation.

Joshua 10:12-13 - Then Joshua spoke to the Lord in the day when the LORD delivered up the Amorites before the children of Israel, and he said in the sight of Israel: "Sun, stand still over Gibeon; And Moon, in the Valley of Aijalon." So the sun stood still, And the moon stopped, Till the people had revenge Upon their enemies. Is this not written in the Book of Jasher? So the sun stood still in the midst of heaven, and did not hasten to go down for about a whole day.

Joshua fulfilled his apostolic mandate and gave each tribe their inheritance as God had instructed him. The Lord also gave God's people rest from their enemies.

6. The apostolic fulfillment of Naomi

(Apostolic mandate: make a way for the Messiah.)

The life story of Naomi is one of the most profound in the Bible. To a theologian it may seem unthinkable to see Naomi as someone with an apostolic mantel.

Naomi and her husband were Hebrews but lived in Moab, probably to pursue better economic opportunities. Both their sons married women from Moab.

Naomi's husband died and then both her sons died. Naomi decided to move back to Israel and advised her two daughters-in-law to stay in Moab and remarry, as they were still young.

The one agreed with Naomi, but the other one, Ruth, did not and told Naomi that she would go with her mother-in-law to Israel.

Naomi was worried that Ruth would waste her opportunities by going to Israel. But Ruth saw her prophetic destiny in Naomi.

People will see something in you that you cannot see in yourself. They will see the hope for their own future and they will hold onto you even though you may not have achieved a lot. In the natural, it would seem that Naomi achieved nothing spiritually but Ruth saw something in her and would not be separated from Naomi.

Ruth 1:11 - But Naomi said, "Turn back, my daughters; why will you go with me? Are there still sons in my womb, that they may be your husbands?

Naomi tried once again to dissuade Ruth from travelling with her to Israel. She told Ruth that she could not produce any more sons from her womb and that everything that she could fulfill had been fulfilled. In other words, she said she could give Ruth nothing, but Ruth saw her divine fulfillment in Naomi.

The Book of Ruth is one of the most powerful apostolic books in the Bible. It was written between the time of the judges and the time of the kings of Israel.

God was preparing Israel for a new season that would see them cry out for a king. I believe the church is in a similar season. We are in a transition period and have come from a past season, but we are looking for our King. I believe there is a cry in the church for the King of kings and the Lord of lords to appear and God is going to use an apostolic mantle on His people which will usher in His Kingdom.

2 Peter 3:12 - Looking for and hastening the coming of the day of God, because of which the heavens will be dissolved, being on fire, and the elements will melt with fervent heat?

The Book of Ruth is a type and shadow of where we are today.

When they returned to Israel together, Naomi became very active in Ruth's life. Through Naomi's influence, Ruth marries Boaz, who is a descendant of Abraham and Judah, and gives birth to a son called Obed.

Can you remember in this story when Naomi told Ruth she has no more sons in her womb? Well, read this verse:

Ruth 4:17 - Also the neighbor women gave him a name, saying, "There is a son born to Naomi." And they called his name Obed. He is the father of Jesse, the father of David.

When you think you can produce nothing more, God has new surprises in store for you!

● ● ●

Because Naomi was faithful, God placed a son in her womb for Ruth! It may not come the way we think in our natural mind, but God has many surprising ways to use us fruitfully.

Naomi would never have thought that there were sons in her dead womb that would birth King David and all the other great kings of Israel who would eventually birth Jesus of Nazareth born through Joseph and Mary. Never limit God. Never allow natural circumstances to speak death to you. Naomi thought she had reached her fulfillment, but God had something better. God has something better for you.

7. The apostolic fulfillment of David

(Apostolic mandate: access the future.)

The apostolic anointing upon David's life took him from a lowly position as a shepherd boy to the royal palaces in Jerusalem. God anointed David to be king over Israel, but the journey to the throne was a long arduous one which took him twenty years to fulfill. Although we are anointed for great things, God will take us on a long journey to equip, train, and prepare us for our destination. That is one of the characteristics of the apostolic anointing.

David overcame the limitations of the Law and found a door into God's presence through praise and worship. He accessed the grace of God even before Jesus fulfilled the Law. The apostolic anointing not only took him into the presence of God, but fast forwarded him into the future where He enjoyed the benefits of the

New Covenant hundreds of years before it was established.

Although his enemies tried relentlessly to kill him, God always hid David supernaturally and he was able to survive every time. This should encourage us because although we have a vicious determined enemy, God will always shelter us and protect us especially when we are obedient to His call on our lives and when we worship in His presence.

God is looking for a generation of believers who will access the secrets of heaven so that they can be prepared for future events. The apostolic anointing can take us into the future and allow us to see what He has prepared for us. That is what He did for David and Paul.

David fulfilled his apostolic mandate by firmly formulating the pattern for worship, establishing the Kingdom of God in Israel, and opening the way for the King of kings to be born in Jerusalem.

God gave David the pattern for the temple which he passed onto his son Solomon as an inheritance.

8. The apostolic fulfillment of Solomon

(Apostolic mandate: bring heaven on earth.)

God anointed Solomon with a Spirit of wisdom which made a way for God's people to enjoy peace, safety, and freedom.

But before Solomon could begin with his apostolic mandate, he had to confront and deal with certain people who were close to his father

David. Many believers are unable to advance in their calling because there are obstacles that have to be removed before they can move forward with God.

Solomon had to deal with four people who were obstacles to the peace and prosperity promised for Israel through Solomon's apostolic leadership:

- His brother Adonijah, who had appointed himself as King of Israel
- Abiathar the priest, who had betrayed King David
- Joab, the head of the army of Israel, who had defected from King David and shed innocent blood
- Shimei, who cursed King David

Only once these people were dealt with, could King Solomon begin his legacy.

1 Kings 2:12 - Then Solomon sat on the throne of his father David; and his kingdom was firmly established.

The apostolic anointing on Solomon's life showcased a pattern of God's Kingdom of peace, abundance, power, and favor. Great men and women were drawn to him because of God's favor and blessings on his kingdom and they travelled great distances to see for themselves how God's blessing was upon King Solomon and the whole nation of Israel.

The favor and anointing of God on His church in these last days will empower us to enter nations and release provision, healing, miracles, and the good news of the Kingdom.

Solomon fulfilled his apostolic mandate by transforming the kingdom of Israel from one of war and strife to love, peace, and wealth.

9. The apostolic fulfillment of Esther

(Apostolic mandate: risk everything for God's people.)

God used Esther apostolically to save the Jews from extinction. Around 500 years before Jesus, King Ahasuerus ruled over one hundred and twenty seven provinces from India to Ethiopia. The Jews were free to return to Jerusalem after their seventy years of captivity, but many of them chose to stay in Persia.

The king chose Esther as his queen but did not know that she was a Jew. Haman was a royal vizier to the king and hated the Jews. He devised a plan to annihilate all the Jews who were living in the Persian empire and obtained the King's seal of approval to carry out his evil scheme.

Queen Esther was directed by her uncle Mordecai to petition the king to overturn the the ruling and together they called on the Jews to fast for three days in order to interceded to God for salvation.

She then took the bold initiative to approach the king and reveal her true identity which could have endangered her life and royal position in the kingdom. But Esther found favor in the sight of the King and overturned the decree. He also had Haman hanged. As a result, Esther saved the nation from destruction and Mordecai was promoted to Prime Minister.

Esther risked her royal position as queen of one of the largest empires in the world at the time in order to fulfill God's plan for the nation.

10. The apostolic fulfillment of Elijah

(Apostolic mandate: turn nations to God.)

The life of Elijah was full of miracles and the manifest power of God. The apostolic anointing on his life brought him before kings and world authorities where he challenged and confronted them without any fear.

The Spirit of God was upon Elijah and he was anointed to turn the hearts of people to God. His entire life was spent focusing people on the one and only true God - the God of Abraham, Isaac, and Jacob.

This same Spirit was upon John the Baptist. Jesus referred to him as a type of Elijah because his purpose was to exhort men and women to repent of their sins and commit their lives to the Lord.

Malachi 4: 5-6 - Behold, I will send you Elijah the prophet before the coming of the great and dreadful day of the LORD: And he shall turn the heart of the fathers to the children, and the heart of the children to their fathers, lest I come and smite the earth with a curse.

This same apostolic anointing will come upon the church in this last season of the church age as we prepare ourselves to go to the nations and turn hearts to Jesus. Many Christians are involved with turning people against the church, or to rebel against church leaders. Others become obsessed with doctrines that turn people away from the true message of love and salvation. But all that is about to change as God's people begin to position themselves for God's glory and purposes.

Elijah exhorted the people to make a quality decision for God and not to be stuck between two options.

He also became an apostolic voice to nature when he stopped rain from falling on the earth for three years and it was that same voice that ended the drought. We will function in this same anointing and need to realize how important our gift is to the Kingdom and begin to see to what measure God will use us if we submit to His plans.

Elijah fulfilled his apostolic mandate by raising up a spiritual successor and being transported bodily into the presence of God.

11. The apostolic fulfillment of Jesus

(Apostolic mandate: salvation and eternal life to all.)

Jesus was sent by God to bring salvation to mankind. He presented the love of His Father to a fallen world with no hope.

Hebrews 3:1 - Therefore, holy brethren, partakers of the heavenly calling, consider the

Apostle and High Priest of our confession, Christ Jesus.

Jesus was the Sent One, the Apostle and High Priest of our confession. He started out His ministry after being anointed by the Holy Spirit at the Jordan and preached the Kingdom of God.

He was God who became flesh and identified with the sufferings and bondages placed on God's beloved creation through the works of the devil.

Moses came down from the mountain with two tablets of stone which incorporated the Law. Jesus fulfilled the law by giving us two commandments by which to live and that is to love God and others.

Jesus fulfilled His apostolic mandate by shedding His blood on the cross for our sins, defeating all the power of the enemy, overcoming the grave, giving authority to His children, ascending into heaven, and taking His place at the right hand of the Father.

Because He finished what His Father wanted Him to do, men and women now have the opportunity to accept Him and become part of His family through the blood of His Son Jesus.

Jesus is in control of everything and is definitely in control of what is about to manifest in the last days. That is why Paul teaches us not to be in fear but to be encouraged, especially when we see the signs of trouble coming in the world.

Colossians 1:17 - And He is before all things, and in Him all things consist.

The things that are about to manifest in the last days will not catch Jesus by surprise. All this is part of His plan and the end time church is about to be empowered with an apostolic mandate and they will work with God in order to fulfill God's purposes.

Like Noah, we are living in perilous times, but we are about to see His glory and His name lifted high!

12. The apostolic fulfillment of Paul

(Apostolic mandate: define the church age.)

The Apostle Paul's ministry was phenomenal. After Pentecost the church had to be organized, structured, and mentored according to the pattern of heaven and through the apostolic anointing on his life, Paul was able to access all the secrets God had for the church which he implemented successfully.

For example, before Pentecost, there was no understanding of:

- the church
- tongues
- walking in the Spirit
- the operation of the gifts of the Spirit
- the five-fold ministry
- the ministry gifts
- the manifestation gifts of the Spirit
- the fruits of the Spirit

- elders, deacons, bishops, overseers, and other church offices
- grace and the law
- faith
- salvation of the Gentile nations
- planting of churches
- missions outside the nation of Israel
- husbands, wives, and children
- the return of Jesus in the clouds
- communion
- types and shadows in the Old Testament perfected in the New Covenant
- and much, much more

Paul wrote two thirds of the New Testament and the revelation that the church received through his anointing has guided the church for the past two thousand years. The dispensation of the church differed totally from the way God engaged Israel as described in the Old Testament. When the church was birthed, they did not have a manual to live by as the Old Testament on its own would not have been relevant.

We must also consider that Paul never met Jesus while He was on earth. He was taught by the Holy Spirit who revealed God's plan for the church. He was passionate about what he believed and could have been very intimidating to the apostles in Jerusalem who had walked with Jesus for the three and a half years of His ministry, yet they did not have the revelation Paul had.

Paul's life is an example to us today because we can gain so much knowledge through intimacy with the Holy Spirit.

Paul took the gospel boldly to the surrounding nations and travelled on many missionary journeys. He suffered great persecution, trials, and temptation, but he fulfilled his apostolic mandate.

2 Timothy 4:7 - I have fought the good fight, I have finished the race, I have kept the faith.

He inspires the true church today and has given us such a great example to follow. The apostolic anointing raised this great leader at a time when God needed him and the same apostolic anointing is about to raise the leaders the church so desperately needs today.

The apostolic anointing on Paul's life brought him into the presence of God in heaven and God took him into the future and showed him the things that God wanted the church to know and do. God also took him into the future and showed him the glory, power, and perfection of the church in the last days.

Pray for the apostolic anointing

God has given us certain signs that confirm we are living in the last generation. We are the generation who are seeing these signs and we will also see an outpouring of the apostolic anointing that will bring the five-fold ministry together to equip the saints of God for the work that lies ahead.

There are two groups of people looking at these events. One group lives in fear, distress, and perplexity. The other lives in hope, power, and love.

Those who love God and live according to His ways will see His glory and witness His mighty plan unfold that will bring the kingdom of darkness to shame and destruction. This is the wrong time to backslide or to become bound with the agendas of this world. This is the time for us to walk closer and closer to Him and to make sure we are doing our part for His Kingdom.

We are the covenant sons and daughters of the living God. We do not have a spirit of fear but we have a spirit of power, love, and a sound mind. We are able to use our anointed minds to think rationally and to make the right choices as we process what is going on in the world today. It is certainly not a pretty picture. But we have a hope and a future even when disasters strike the earth and when the money fails.

Matthew 24:37-42 - But as the days of Noah were, so also will the coming of the Son of Man be. For as in the days before the flood, they were eating and drinking, marrying and giving in marriage, until the day that Noah entered the ark, and did not know until the flood came and took them all away, so also will the coming of the Son of Man be. Then two men will be in the field: one will be taken and the other left. Two women will be grinding at the mill: one will be taken and the other left. Watch therefore, for you do not know what hour your Lord is coming.

This is so true as we see the spirit of mockery in the world today. As Noah was preaching and preparing the people for the coming judgment of God, they laughed at him and rejected his message. As he continued to tell people in the world over many, many years of the impending doom they would face if they did not repent, the clouds began to gather on the horizon.

But they were enjoying a life of pleasure and partying and did not want to change. There are people who do not want to be inconvenienced by the message of the Kingdom. When the destruction came, only Noah and his family together with two species of every creature were saved.

As Jesus prophesied, we are living in the same days as Noah lived in. People are more concerned with enjoying life with its pleasures and do not want to bow their knees to Jesus. But disaster is coming. Hell was never made for people. It was made for the devil and his rebellious followers. We as children of God need to ask ourselves whether we are in the right place.

Dark clouds are gathering on the horizon and great trouble is on its way. We need to ask ourselves whether we will be in a place of safety or whether we be exposed to the elements that will bring disaster and death.

The end is coming and we must make sure we are in the right place to receive the apostolic anointing. God will protect His people no matter what is coming on the earth.

Hear this apostolic message for God's people who are alive in this season:

"If My people would only stop doubting and once again start believing and if My people would not look to the natural but look to My supernatural ability, then they will come to fulfillment and be complete. Many people reach their fulfillment but your fulfillment is not My fulfillment, says the Lord. I want to take you to a greater place and many times, I will work through families so that nations can be blessed."

This message is for you today. Pray this prayer over your life:

"Lord, the time of my fulfillment has come. Lord, you have called me for the supernatural and the impossible. There is still hope for me because I am alive and the final chapter of my life has not yet been written."

Keep your mind focused on the Lord and He will keep you in perfect peace and remember – it is not over until it is over!

Chapter 9

Preparing For Battle

There were thousands of followers of Jesus that missed Him at Pentecost because they did not have an apostolic revelation of God's Kingdom. When you simply follow the crowds, you could end up following someone who is either going nowhere or going to a bad place.

We should all have a prophetic understanding of where we are going in order to fulfill our destiny. God's prophetic clock tells us which season we are living in. We need to know what God's plan is for our generation and pray earnestly that God will give us a road map to where He wants us to go. When you follow God, you will always land up in a good place and you will never be lost or confused.

God's people cannot read tea leaves and we can certainly not look into crystal balls. Of course, there are people who rely on this kind of stuff to direct them, but that is not God's way of doing things and it will take you to the wrong place. Your life is precious and you cannot afford to take a wrong turn in your life.

We need to find the mind of Christ because He alone has all the information and knowledge for every season. We need to know what He is saying and allow Him to direct our footsteps into the future. He knows what He wants to do in these final years that are left on the earth and only He knows how things are going to turn out. Jesus is in control of everything and when you follow Him, you will always be ahead of those who do not rely on His leading.

There are a number of apostolic exhortations that can help us in the difficult times ahead.

1. Look at the signs

We know we are living in the last days because the Bible has given us certain signs that confirm this belief. We do not have to look for any more signs because most of them have already come to pass. The last sign that must be fulfilled is the mass worldwide evangelization that will bring in the final harvest of souls into God's Kingdom. Once that has been completed, the end will come.

Matthew 24:14 - And this gospel of the kingdom will be preached in all the world as a witness to all the nations, and then the end will come.

Let us have a look at some of the signs the Bible has told us about.

Matthew 24:6-13 - And you will hear of wars and rumors of wars. See that you are not troubled; for all these things must come to pass, but the end is not yet. For nation will rise against nation, and kingdom against kingdom. And there will be famines, pestilences, and earthquakes in various places. All these are the beginning of sorrows. "Then they will deliver you up to tribulation and kill you, and you will be hated by all nations for My name's sake. And then many will be offended, will betray one another, and will hate one another. Then many false prophets will rise up and deceive many. And because lawlessness will abound, the love of many will grow cold. But he who endures to the end shall be saved.

a. Earthquakes

Almost every week or so, we hear of earthquakes which are causing enormous panic and alarm worldwide. The world is on constant alert for the signs of tsunamis that have wreaked havoc on many continents.

b. Conflict

Almost every week or so, we hear of new conflicts that have flared up causing war between nations and people groups. One of the major causes of these new outbreaks of war is the search for shrinking resources such as water, oil, minerals, and fertile land.

c. Famine

We hear about famine almost every day as agricultural land becomes more and more scarce especially because of climate change. Entire communities that used to feed themselves for centuries now have to rely on food distribution and this is becoming more

• • •

and more expensive for food organizations to provide.

d. Incurable diseases

Aids has been an uncontrollable pandemic which cannot be cured. It has destroyed entire communities and no nation has been spared.

e. Financial troubles

Almost every nation on earth is stressed out because of the financial crisis that has crippled so many economies worldwide. Europe has been hit the hardest and as they deal with a financial crisis in one country in the Eurozone, another nation suffers a similar fate. It is becoming worse every day and is threatening to break up the Europeans union. This will make a way for the antichrist to emerge and lead Europe and the rest of the world out of their financial mess by formulating a workable austerity plan that will rescue them for a season. That time is now and he can appear at any moment.

f. Lawlessness

Lawlessness and violence has become the norm all over the world even in nations that have experienced very low crime rates in the past. All that is changing. Ten years ago, homes in America did not need to be protected. But today, armed response companies are operational in most cities and most households have installed alarm systems.

Today there are so many governments who have become lawless and perpetrators of violence and do not care what the world thinks as they go about slaughtering their own people. They have become a law unto themselves and ignore orders that are issued by their courts as well as indictments by the International Criminal Court.

2. The political landscape

We need to have an understanding of how the political landscape will change because the way nations have been organizing themselves will change. We have observed how the European Union has come about and consolidated its power base.

If we are to believe God's Word, we should know that all the nations will move towards a one-world government.

The European Union has been reasonably successful in uniting nations politically and this model could also be used to bring many more nations together in a one-world system of government. It may seem unthinkable for nations such as Russia, China, Israel and other Middle East countries to agree to a one-world government.

But this could come about mainly by the will of the people. We have seen in the past few years how the people in Libya, Egypt, and Tunisia have overturned their governments by the shear will and determination of the people.

The voice of the people are shouting for equal rights and they want human rights to be upheld. Discontent could bring about massive change worldwide especially in countries that are still ruled by dictators. Perhaps it will be the people and not governments that will usher in a one-world government. Governments that resist change will fall no matter how powerful they are. We have seen that happen with the Soviet Union when the iron curtain fell in one day. Once this happens, nations will begin to realize that they have very little differences between them and they may find it beneficial to form a one-world system of government.

The moment this happens, the Antichrist will make his appearance and will head the nations for a time. But he will not be democratic and will break all his promises.

Initially he will be able to sort out the financial mess in the world and one of the things he will introduce is a single currency and a cashless society. To make it more convenient, buying and selling will be conducted by his mark which will be made either on a person's right hand or on the forehead. Without the mark, no one will be able to buy or sell. But the Bible tells us that anyone who receives this mark will be cast into the lake of fire.

He will also create a massive statue of himself and will demand that men and women bow down to him.

Most Christians believe that the church will be raptured at this time and will not have to face these issues. But even if the Lord delays His coming and we are around to see a part or all of these things, God is able to protect us and to provide for as in the same way He provided food, clothing, and shelter for the Israelites in the desert.

• • •

3. The mighty harvest

God is about to empower the church who will come together in unity and will work together apostolically to bring in a supernatural harvest of souls in every nation and their future will be decided on the streets.

Matthew 24:14 - And this gospel of the kingdom will be preached in all the world as a witness to all the nations, and then the end will come.

This event must still take place and will come about once the offices of the apostle and prophet are restored to the church which will bring the five-fold ministry together. They will equip the believers and organize the church into a strong fighting force. The saints of God will go out in power and bind the strongman over each and every nation and rescue the unsaved from the clutches of Satan.

This is going to be done supernaturally as so many nations and people groups on the earth are bound by false religions which is at the very root of their culture and difficult to break. God's people will fight a holy war against God's enemy, the devil.

Matthew 11:12 - And from the days of John the Baptist until now the Kingdom of heaven suffers violence, and the violent take it by force.

This prophecy is about to be fulfilled supernaturally. The Kingdom of God will be expressed through a united church flowing with an apostolic anointing. It is not united now but God is about to bring it into a mature fighting force that will advance God's Kingdom violently and without any fear.

The five-fold ministry will be complete and will work together in equipping the believers for the work of the ministry. They will receive divine strategy from God and will be positioned at the right place at the right time.

Ephesians 4:11-12 - And He Himself gave some to be apostles, some prophets, some evangelists, and some pastors and teachers, for the equipping of the saints for the work of ministry, for the edifying of the body of Christ..

This is a prophetic word for the church and it will be fulfilled very soon. The five-fold leaders will give the church weapons of war and the church will be united as one army which will be in the image of Jesus. When the devil sees the church, he will see Jesus who defeated him two thousand years ago.

There is going to be a yoke destroying soul winning preaching revival that is going to sweep millions into the Kingdom of God and the whole earth will be filled with the knowledge of the glory of God.

Be prepared

God is going to give us supernatural ability and Satan will not be able to touch us. We will release healings, signs and wonders, miracles, and break the chains of bondage wherever we go. We have the name of Jesus in our mouths and we are going to advance into the enemy's territory with great authority and power and take back what he has stolen.

God is going to use the following people in the last days:

- God is going to use men
- God is going to use women
- God is going to use young people and even children
- God is going to use old people
- God is going to use people that have been racially marginalized
- God is going to use those who have been rejected by society

The greater glory of God is going to fill God's people and their faces will shine like the face of Moses. Can you imagine an army of believers marching towards the enemy with their faces shining? The church is once again going to be strong and will take back territory from the enemy. The wealth of the unrighteous is going to come back to God's people. We are living in very exciting times. How wrong we were to believe that the Christian life is dull and dreary!

Be separate

We need to separate ourselves from the world if we want God to use us. If we want to be part of this great move of God, we will need to distance ourselves from those things that exalt Satan and embrace the things that exalt God. Commit everything to Jesus and do not follow the devil because he will lead you right into the flames of hell. But remember, God has not put you on this earth so that you can burn with the devil but that you can burn with the fire of God!

Work things out so that you can be ready to be used by God. Everything is going to change in a day and when that happens make sure you do not find yourself on the wrong side. Do not play with God because the time is now.

Philippian 2:12 - Therefore, my beloved, as you have always obeyed, not as in my presence only, but now much more in my absence, workout your own salvation with fear and trembling;

Chapter 10

Characteristics Of The Apostolic Anointing

In order to have a true understanding of the apostolic anointing, we must know that God intervenes in the affairs of this world and He uses His anointed vessels to accomplish His plans.

Today, everything is opposed to God. Sadly, a large section of the church today can be regarded as anti-God because of certain beliefs that have been erased and taught which go against God's ways.

But there is good news. God's glory is coming and the church will be changed by the glory and presence of God.

The church is about to be transformed by the Spirit of God and will be made ready for the Bridegroom.

Although the church is not there yet, the bride will match the Bridegroom in power, perfection, and glory.

God is going to touch the church supernaturally and the apostolic anointing will do the supernatural work necessary to bring about the transformation.

Traditionally, the church has always comprised of different leaders at different levels. The early church had overseers, elders, deacons, bishops, shepherd, and the five-fold ministry to structure it and to ensure its orderly function.

This multi-level hierarchy of leadership has persisted throughout the two thousand year history of the church and is applicable to a large degree to the 21st century church.

But the apostolic anointing is going to bring about a complete change in the leadership structure of the church in order to prepare for its role in the last days.

Ephesians 4:11-13 - And He Himself gave some to be apostles, some prophets, some evangelists, and some pastors and teachers, for the equipping of the saints for the work of ministry, for the edifying of the body of Christ, till we all come to the unity of the faith and of the knowledge of the Son of God, to a perfect man, to the measure of the stature of the fullness of Christ.

This is a passage of Scripture that is widely used today, but when we look at the intended end result, it is largely prophetic. There are only going to be two groups of people in the future church which will consist of the priests and the people or the five-fold ministry and the workers.

1. The apostolic anointing will restore the church leadership

These are the apostles, prophets, evangelists, pastors, and teachers whose sole task is to equip the children of God so that they can do the work of the ministry. That means the five-fold ministers will not do the work of the ministry as is the case today. They will be equipping the saints to do this work.

There are many Christians who believe it is the apostles who will bring about the changes, but in reality it will be the inclusion of the apostles joining with the other four ministry offices that will bring this about.

The apostolic anointing does not refer to the office of the apostle, but rather to the equipping anointing that flows when all five of these ministry gifts work together as one. This will occur once God restores the office of the apostle, as they are the missing link at the present time. It does not mean that they are superior in any way. They are simply missing from the group of five and once God restores them to the body, the apostolic anointing will flow through these five ministry offices and the church will begin its journey to perfection.

No matter how hard we try to find the perfect church, this will not happen until the apostolic anointing is released onto the church. Christians wander from church to church seeking a church that is truly operating in power, unity, and love - but their search is in vain. That church does not yet exist on the earth. The time is not yet but it is about to be birthed.

They are Christ's gifts of leaders to His church. Their responsibility is to lead the church and to train the members for ministry. These ministries are given to the body of Christ as a gift. It must be clearly understood that a gift is not earned. For this reason, these five-fold offices cannot be earned. No one can appoint another person into these offices. The Holy Spirit may use the church leadership to confirm the call of God on an individual but they cannot decide to appoint a person into any one of the five-fold ministries.

The ministry gifts are appointed by God and not by the choice of men. Unlike in the Old Testament, this gift is not inherited from one generation of a particular family to the next. The genealogy regarding spiritual inheritance finished with Christ. For this reason there are no recorded inheritances of the anointing from any of the apostles to their children.

Christ is the head of His church and it is He alone who determines who is called into any of the five-fold gifts. Each person is divinely endowed with the spiritual gifts necessary to carry out that calling. All the offices of the five-fold ministry are meant for different functions and for different purposes and are to be performed by people who are chosen and anointed by God.

Each member of the five-fold team on their own is not apostolic. That means even the apostle on his or her own is not apostolic. When the five come together, the apostolic church will be birthed. That is God's plan for the leadership of His glorious church.

2. The apostolic anointing will equip the workers

This is the second level that will operate in the church. Those in the office of the five-fold ministry will not do the work of the ministry. The ordinary members will be equipped by the five-fold and they will go out into the world and do the work of the ministry.

The purpose of the gifts is to build up the church. The Spirit manifests Himself through these gifts to edify the church and demonstrate the reality of God to unbelievers. The gifts and the ministries of the gifts of the Holy Spirit have the purpose to build the church in unity and love for Christ.

They will work in unity and each person will know what their function is in the body. They will have an external focus rather than trying to compete for position and recognition in the internal structures of the church as it is today. They will be able to exercise their ministry gift because they will apply it externally. They will be armed by the five-fold ministry with the tools of the trade and with weapons of war.

Each will operate in their gift and the corporate anointing that will flow because of their unity will allow both groups to be effective globally.

They will come together as the church and be trained and they will all have a common goal and purpose. No one will be able operate on their own or in isolation. The church will function supernaturally with these two levels of ministry and will be unstoppable.

3. The apostolic anointing will define the order of the church

No ministry will be performed by anyone without being connected with the five-fold apostolic anointing. The five-fold will work together and all five working together will release the apostolic anointing which will bring the body into unity and perfection. If any one of the gifts are missing, the anointing will no longer flow.

Psalm 133:1-3 - A Song of Ascents. Of David. Behold, how good and how pleasant it is For brethren to dwell together in unity! It is like the precious oil upon the head, Running down on the beard, The beard of Aaron, Running down on the edge of his garments. It is like the dew of Hermon, Descending upon the mountains of Zion; For there the LORD commanded the blessing-Life forevermore.

There will not be an emphasis on bringing people to church to listen to a sermon on a Sunday. It will be a place of preparation and ministering outside the walls of the church.

The old way of church will no longer be relevant because there will be no more grace for it and no fruit will come from it.

Church leaders work tirelessly to bring their churches to a "fullness" in terms of the number of members attending the services but the focus will change to a fullness of Christ. This is what we can expect to see :

- The church will operate in unity of faith
- Christ will be the Head of the church
- The church will look like Christ
- The church will be permeated by God's glory
- The church will be holy and without spot or blemish
- The church will be mature
- The church will have one doctrine

When we look at the church today, this transformation seems unthinkable. God is looking for men and women who will believe the prophetic word over Christ's beautiful bride and speak life into this dead institution by faith and believe that the church can rise again and form a mighty army that will do the impossible.

Ezekiel 37:1-10 - The hand of the LORD came upon me and brought me out in the Spirit of the LORD, and set me down in the midst of the valley; and it was full of bones. Then He caused me to pass by them all around, and behold, there were very many in the open valley; and indeed they were very dry. And He said to me, "Son of man, can these bones live?" So I answered, "O Lord GOD, You know." Again He said to me, "Prophesy to these bones, and say to them, 'O dry bones, hear the word of the LORD! Thus says the Lord GOD to these bones: "Surely I will cause breath to enter into you, and you shall live.

• • •

I will put sinews on you and bring flesh upon you, cover you with skin and put breath in you; and you shall live. Then you shall know that I am the LORD." ' " So I prophesied as I was commanded; and as I prophesied, there was a noise, and suddenly a rattling; and the bones came together, bone to bone. Indeed, as I looked, the sinews and the flesh came upon them, and the skin covered them over; but there was no breath in them. Also He said to me, "Prophesy to the breath, prophesy, son of man, and say to the breath, 'Thus says the Lord GOD: "Come from the four winds, O breath, and breathe on these slain, that they may live." ' " So I prophesied as He commanded me, and breath came into them, and they lived, and stood upon their feet, an exceedingly great army.

Like Ezekiel, God is challenging us today so that every part of the body can come together in life and purpose. Let us begin to prophecy and speak life over the church so that God will accelerate its purpose and advance His plans.

Ephesians 4:16 - From whom the whole body, joined and knit together by what every joint supplies, according to the effective working by which every part does its share, causes growth of the body for the edifying of itself in love.

4. The apostolic anointing will implement God's plan

Matthew 24:14 - And this gospel of the kingdom will be preached in all the world as a witness to all the nations, and then the end will come.

This is the purpose of the glorious church and this will be its mission and focus. When we begin to work with the plan of God, His power and favor will be released upon us and we will be included in His plan.

5. The apostolic anointing will reflect Christ

Ephesians 4:13-16 - Till we all come to the unity of the faith and of the knowledge of the Son of God, to a perfect man, to the measure of the stature of the fullness of Christ...

Those who are wise will be well positioned and waiting. When the enemy sees the bride, he will see Christ who defeated him at Calvary and there will be no more fight in him. At the sight of the bride, the enemy will flee and leave the spoils of war for us to take. Whose side will you be on? That is a choice that you have to make.

Still to be revealed

The true apostolic ministry has not yet been fully revealed and is a prophetic expectation that the church is looking for. The fact that certain Christian leaders are appointed as apostles or carry the title of apostle does not necessarily imply that they are functioning in the apostolic anointing.

Although many apostles today are planting churches and fathering many congregations, the apostolic anointing is primarily needed to bring the church into unity and in the full stature of Christ. The church is about to be transformed by the Spirit of God so that it can be ready for the purpose that God has for it in this season. The bride will match the

Bridegroom in power, perfection, and glory. That is the mandate of the five-fold ministry.

There are many who say that the apostolic age ended when the last of the apostles died. Without being controversial, I tend to believe that because the early apostles set the momentum, standard, and order for the church to follow and this has carried the church for two thousand years. Over this period, the church strayed from its original blueprint many times and that is why God sent a number of revivals to bring it back to the original 1st century plan.

The DNA of the church has not changed since its birth two thousand years ago and the strengths and weaknesses that they have experienced from the beginning are still experienced today in the 21st century, as summed up by Jesus when describing the seven church types in the book of Revelation.

If this is true, then there is no need for apostles to continue with the foundations of the present church. It can then also be argued, that the full five-fold ministry as mentioned by Paul in Ephesians 4, has never been in existence, because if that were the case, the church would have matured long ago and come into unity. Each of these offices function today in their individual capacities, some in a greater measure than others. But when they work together supernaturally, the apostolic anointing will be released and will achieve what God has planned for the coming transformation of the church.

God is about to do something new because the church is going to be glorious and will look like Christ. Throughout history, God has always raised up men and women with an apostolic anointing to usher in each new phase of His Kingdom and we are about to see this happen once again in our generation. It cannot be initiated by the will of men and women by trying to re-organize the church into a five-fold structure. This can only come about in God's timing and by His Spirit.

We are living in a prophetic season similar to that of John the Baptist, who proclaimed that a new season was about to break forth upon the earth. We need to prepare ourselves for this coming move and we must be ready to accept it no matter in what form it is presented. The religious communities missed their Messiah because they did not expect Him to come as a baby born by a woman. They were good people and had kept the faith alive for many hundreds of years and eagerly awaited the coming of the promised Messiah. Yet they missed Him!

Many thousands of followers missed the supernatural outpouring at Pentecost because they thought their dreams died when Jesus was crucified. Out of the five hundred who saw the resurrected Jesus with their own eyes, only one hundred and twenty waited by faith in the Upper Room.

"This is a warning to the church today. We need to be ready for this new season because it is upon us. Jesus instructed His disciples not to leave Jerusalem, but to wait in the Upper Room

for the new season. They did this, but during those ten days, they appointed an apostle by casting lots which was not what Jesus told them to do. In this last hour of the church age, we need to be careful not to create structures that pre-empt what God is planning to do, because it can be a futile exercise in the flesh" – A revelation received by Pastor Rakesh Ramdas, my spiritual son in the Lord.

Chapter 11

Doing The Work Of The Kingdom

The entire word of God is prophetic because it is futuristic.

Amos 3:7 - Surely the Lord GOD does nothing, Unless He reveals His secret to His servants the prophets.

We know that we can prepare boldly for what is coming because Jesus gave us the prophetic signs. He told us what we should look out for and we know that we are living in the last days because prophetically the Bible has shown us where the church will be in the future. We know that it will end glorious and will end strong and not weak. The Laodicean church is one of the seven churches that Jesus spoke about in the last days but it will not be the final church because the last church will be united and strong and will grow into the full stature of Jesus.

God is equipping and preparing His children for great and mighty things and we will finish strong. We will take the nations for Jesus by preaching the gospel to the ends of the earth. The devil has already been defeated and although he will exert great power on the earth, his reign of terror will end in the lake of fire.

The entire Word of God is prophetic, but it is also apostolic because the word "apostolic" is a doing word.

James 1:22 - But be doers of the word, and not hearers only, deceiving yourselves.

This is one of the most relevant apostolic verses of Scripture in the Bible. The apostolic means we are required to do something. The apostle is a person who performs the word in deed. At Pentecost, the disciples became apostles because they were anointed to do ministry. Jesus' ministry was apostolic because of what He did.

Acts 10:38 - How God anointed Jesus of Nazareth with the Holy Spirit and with power, who went about doing good and healing all who were oppressed by the devil, for God was with Him.

When you are busy working for God you are apostolic. The definition of an apostle is "one who is sent to represent another." We are sent by God to represent heaven on earth. We are the answer to a distressed world.

The true definition of the apostolic ministry is "someone who is anointed by God to perform a supernatural task on the earth which will add to God's Kingdom." It implies that we can all be apostolic. God has always been building His Kingdom over thousands and thousands of years. To God, building His Kingdom or building His church is the same thing.

There are some terminologies in the Word that may change. The first time the word "apostle" was used was in the New Testament. It was never mentioned in the Old Testament, but its meaning carries the same function throughout the Old and New Testaments because God has always sent men and women to represent Him and to perform work for Him.

There are anointed people who are doing things in the name of the Lord but they are not sent by God to do whatever they are doing. The Bible speaks about these people who will stand before Him testifying to all the mighty deeds they have done during their time on earth. But Jesus will send them away saying "I never knew you." If we are not sent by God, we will not be acknowledged by Him. It is important to do only what God directs us to do. That is what Jesus did. He never did anything without God's permission.

We cannot solve all the problems in the world, but we should rather wait for God to show us what He wants us to do before we do anything. We also need to know that we are following people who have been sent by God.

God has called us to work with Him and He is building His Kingdom with us and through us.

God is the builder

Colossians 1:16 - For by Him all things were created that are in heaven and that are on earth, visible and invisible, whether thrones or dominions or principalities or powers. All things were created through Him and for Him.

From this we can see the great apostolic power of Jesus as the creator and because He created everything, He has power and authority over what He created. Those who have an apostolic anointing are also creative and the things we build for God are a testimony against the kingdom of darkness.

Matthew 16:18 - And I also say to you that you are Peter, and on this rock I will build My church, and the gates of Hades shall not prevail against it.

What God builds defeats the devil and the things we build with God cannot be destroyed by the enemy. If you want to ensure the devil's defeat, build with the Lord because what you build will defeat his demonic assignments against you. To be apostolic means building something that exalts God and overcomes the enemy.

Anything that was built by God and His workers in the Old Testament, is apostolic and anything built by God and His workers since then, is apostolic. God has not yet finished building His Kingdom. For example, He has yet to create a new heaven and a new earth which He will do sometime in the future.

That is part of His future plans and we are part of His present plans. That is why we need to have the blueprint for today. We cannot use the blueprints of the church of yesterday, because God has moved on from there and is building something different today. The plans used by any previous generation cannot be used today because we are involved with building something different. God is in another place today and we have to do what God wants us to do. We should also not build anything without a blueprint from heaven or else we could be building something that He does not want.

God has anointed every one of us to build apostolically.

Start with the foundation

God is the creator and we are created in His image to create. When we talk about building with God it means that we are creating with Him. Even though He created the heavens and earth, He has never stopped the creative process and we are part of that process. He has given us a prophetic power to create things with our mouths.

Everything we see in the physical or natural environment responds to words. That is the way God's creation is designed. Words which line up with God's Word have power and when these words are applied to God's creation, there will be a response.

God has given us the ability and the authority to frame our world with His Words. Prophetic words have power and can be spoken into our circumstances in order to shape our world so that it reflects the majesty and power of God's Kingdom.

But there is a time to speak and a time to do things. That is why we need the apostolic and prophetic anointing.

Any impressive building will have a cornerstone to show that it is valuable and it usually contains the names of the architect, master builder, and the visionary.

Whatever God builds is valuable and Jesus is the cornerstone of everything He builds. If Jesus is not part of the building it is not worth building. If it is not built by Him it is not His building.

Not everything that is built honors and exalts God. There are buildings that come against the purposes of God. Many of God's pioneers in the Old Testament built altars as a testimony to what God had done for them and God was always the cornerstone of that altar. But those who worshipped false gods would build altars to exalt their gods and these altars opposed the Kingdom of God.

Anything that is not built by God must be broken down and rebuilt. Our lives must exalt God. We are Gods building and there is nothing wrong with starting again if the foundation is not right.

1 Peter 2:6-8 - Therefore it is also contained in the Scripture, "Behold, I lay in Zion a Chief Cornerstone, elect, precious, and he who believes

on Him will by no means be put to shame."
Therefore, to you who believe, He is precious; but
to those who are disobedient, "The stone which
the builders rejected has become the chief
cornerstone," and "a stone of stumbling and a
rock of offense." They stumble, being disobedient
to the word, to which they also were appointed.

God places His name on everything He builds like artists who autograph their paintings. The value is determined by the name on the painting. When Jesus is the cornerstone of our lives it denotes value.

When Jesus is the cornerstone of what we build whether it is our spiritual life, our marriage, our home life, our careers, or our businesses, the name of Jesus will always be a stumbling block to those who oppose Him because the cornerstone will reflect heaven.

God wants everything to be built on His apostolic blueprint so that it can exalt Jesus who is the creator and the greatest example of the apostolic anointing .

Hebrews 3:1 - Therefore, holy brethren,
partakers of the heavenly calling, consider the
Apostle and High Priest of our confession, Christ
Jesus.

God wants every family to have an apostolic blueprint so that they can be built according to His plans with Christ as the cornerstone. When others see the building, God will be given the glory. God wants to be glorified in our families, our ministries, our business, and every aspect of our lives. But He can only be glorified if things are build according to His design. When

His name is on the building, it becomes a stumbling block to the kingdom of darkness, but life and hope to the world.

Every ministry should have an apostolic blueprint if it is to succeed. In order to fulfill our apostolic mandate we need to find the blueprint for the cities and nations that God is giving us to rebuild because anything that has not been built according to how God wants it to be built, must be broken down and rebuilt.

There is nothing wrong with rebuilding because there are things that must be redesigned, restructured, and repositioned so that God can be given the glory. If your life is not offending the kingdom of darkness, it means Jesus is not the cornerstone because the cornerstone will be a rock of offense to everything that refuses to bow to Him.

Cornerstones are laid according to our apostolic build-up anointing. God is going to give us a powerful apostolic mandate and we will build into cities and nations and when the building is complete, Christ is going to be the cornerstone of that city or nation. God wants us to place Christ back into these places.

Revelation 11:15 - Then the seventh angel sounded: And there were loud voices in heaven, saying, "The kingdoms of this world have become the kingdoms of our Lord and of His Christ, and He shall reign forever and ever!"

When Paul and his team ministered in cities, the people were convicted of their sin and brought all their occult books and burnt them in public. There are things that do not exalt Christ that are going to be burned up because of our witness.

Be part of the foundation

When we fulfill an apostolic mandate we become part of the foundation. When we build things for God, He places us into the foundation of that building as a testimony for all eternity.

Revelation 21:12 & 14 - Also she had a great and high wall with twelve gates, and twelve angels at the gates, and names written on them, which are the names of the twelve tribes of the children of Israel: Now the wall of the city had twelve foundations, and on them were the names of the twelve apostles of the Lamb.

The names of twelve tribes and the twelve apostles are etched on the foundations of the New Jerusalem because they contributed to the building. God advanced His Kingdom through the twelve tribes of Israel who possessed the Promised Land and laid the foundation for the nation of Israel and performed their apostolic part.

After Pentecost, He built the church through the early apostles and they laid the foundation for the New Covenant believers to build on and they completed their apostolic part.

Ephesians 2:20 - Having been built on the foundation of the apostles and prophets, Jesus Christ Himself being the chief cornerstone.

What we do for God means something and He remembers the names of those who have worked with Him. God does not merely use your life and resources and then forget about you, but He remembers your name and blesses you and your children up to the third and fourth generation.

When you operate prophetically and apostolically, God will make sure your name is in the foundations for all to see and He will send others to build on that foundation from generation to generation.

When your name is mentioned in heaven perhaps a number of cities or nations will be linked to your name.

2 Corinthians 6:1 - We then, as workers together with Him also plead with you not to receive the grace of God in vain.

Your unique anointing will express itself in your passion. If you have a passion to see people healed, God will use you for healing and we cannot do anything without Christ because He is the source of the anointing.

There are things that need supernatural solutions on earth and those secrets need to be accessed from heaven. Pharaoh needed a supernatural solution for the money that would fail in Egypt and God positioned Joseph with an apostolic anointing who provided the secret solution from heaven. Some problems on earth have solutions that are only found in heaven and are released upon the earth through the apostolic anointing which glorify God.

● ● ●

Chapter 12

Preparing For The Apostolic Anointing

If we really believe in the coming move of God which will birth the church in power, we need to make sure that we have prepared ourselves for this anointing.

Before the Holy Spirit was poured out on the early church, they prepared by separating themselves from everyone and waited patiently in the Upper Room. These were men and women who followed Jesus and had walked away from their careers, businesses, family, and religious community, and waited by faith for the anointing that Jesus promised before He ascended into heaven.

There were so many who followed the ministry of Jesus, but there were only one hundred and twenty who prepared themselves for this visitation and they were the only ones who received God's power and they took this anointing to the nations.

In the same way, we need to set ourselves apart and prepare for the apostolic anointing which will transform the church entirely.

The Parable of the Ten Virgins demonstrates this so vividly. There is a clear difference between the two groups of five virgins whom Jesus referred to in the New Testament. Their story is told in Matthew 25.

The essential difference was that one group of five had the oil of the anointing, and the other group did not. The church has a destiny which will be characterized by the apostolic anointing which will manifest a greater corporate demonstration of God's power.

Preaching, programs, and fellowship can never become a substitute for the anointing of the Holy Spirit. Only through a personal, intimate relationship with God the Holy Spirit can we be empowered to bear fruit that will produce a Kingdom legacy.

1. Study

We must progress spiritually and grow to maturity. A child cannot grow physically without proper food. Good parents are concerned about proper nutrition. They want their children to eat what is good and not what is bad for them.

Likewise, we cannot grow in our gifting without feeding on God's Word. Some Christians believe that they can do without the Bible and only need to wait on God for a prophetic word. But all ministry is based on God's Word and cannot flourish without it.

The apostolic anointing works through the Word. Make sure you know the Word thoroughly in order to be more effective in your anointing.

Study the apostolic anointing evident in the lives of God's leaders and ministers in both the Old and New Testaments.

Read and meditate on the Word of God continuously over and over again. Equip yourself by studying further through a Spirit-filled anointed Bible College.

Training and mentoring is a Biblical concept. In the Old Testament, Elijah and Elisha had groups of prophets that looked to them for leadership.

Jesus trained His disciples who in turn trained other leaders to do the work of the ministry.

To function successfully in the prophetic and apostolic anointing will take years of study, practice, and training to develop to its fullest potential. To be a good steward of the gifts God has given to us, will mean that we will have to invest time and effort in order to increase in the anointing.

Every believer who is sincere about growing in their calling and anointing should submit themselves to an equipping program. They should enroll in ministry training that covers courses that teach all the major themes related to a Spirit-filled ministry environment.

Most growing churches today have training centers or church-based Bible schools which form part of their vision. If you really believe God wants to use you and you have a desire to be used by God, spend two to three years in a local Bible school and prepare yourself for ministry. Many people think that they only need the anointing in order to launch out in ministry, but find themselves hopelessly ill-equipped to deal with the challenges facing them.

Expand your knowledge at every opportunity by reading books and articles related to your gift.

Make sure every doctrine you follow exalts the Lord Jesus and no one else. Ask the Holy Spirit to reveal the truth to you especially when you listen to teachings by others.

2. Choose the right church

Local church government is provided by God to ensure the best conditions possible for each individual to fulfill their ministry.

Many Christians do not join a local church because they think the institution is foolish and unnecessary. However, nothing of spiritual value will be added to your life outside of the local church. Submitting to the leadership of a church activates the power of God for our individual destinies and purposes.

There is no substitute for attending church. Besides it being something that pleases God, it is necessary for the spiritual well-being of God's children.

Hebrews 10:24-25 - And let us consider one another in order to stir up love and good works, not forsaking the assembling of ourselves together, as is the manner of some, but exhorting one another, and so much the more as you see the Day approaching.

There is power that is released when God's people gather together. God will do nothing in your life outside of the institution of His church. One way to put distance between you and the devil is to become part of a local church and to submit to the leadership for spiritual mentoring.

Going to church is a visible, tangible expression of our love and worship toward God. It is where we can gather with other believers to honor Him with service of devotion. Receiving the preaching and teaching of the Word of God increases our faith and builds us up spiritually.

There is the promise of a special visitation of the Lord's presence whenever two or more gather together in the name of Jesus. The Lord honors a gathering in His name by releasing a corporate anointing.

Gathering together also provides fellowship with other believers and is also a matter of obeying God's Word.

God designed this system of accountability for the progress and protection of His flock. This cannot be possible unless God's people are a part of an organized fellowship which has God-ordained leaders.

God places individuals in local churches so that they can submit to their leaders and learn from them. Spiritual development seldom takes place outside the institution of the church.

Becoming skilled in the things of God is not a destination, but a journey of learning. Fundamental to growth is a commitment to a lifelong journey of learning.

Training brings you into contact with people who are on the same journey as you. You can encourage each other, share ideas, and use your gift of prophecy.

> *1 Kings 19:19-21 - So he departed from there, and found Elisha the son of Shaphat, who was plowing with twelve yoke of oxen before him, and he was with the twelfth. Then Elijah passed by him and threw his mantle on him. And he left the oxen and ran after Elijah, and said, "Please let me kiss my father and my mother, and then I will follow you." And he said to him, "Go back again, for what have I done to you?" So Elisha turned back from him, and took a yoke of oxen and slaughtered them and boiled their flesh, using the oxen's equipment, and gave it to the people, and they ate. Then he arose and followed Elijah, and became his servant.*

Elisha was not only Elijah's spiritual apprentice, but he was the only one who caught a double portion of his spirit.

Elijah made three attempts to separate himself from Elisha, but Elisha remained obstinately close to him and followed Elijah wherever he went. These actions must have hurt Elisha, but he was never offended and never became angry.

Too many church members are easily offended with leaders who limit their opportunity for personal growth and development. They leave the church when they feel unnoticed or overlooked.

Whenever you move into new areas of your Christian walk, God will bring new people into your life who can help you and impart knowledge.

You may have to find a new church to take your gifting further if your current church discourages the apostolic and prophetic anointing.

If you want to prepare yourself for the coming anointing, prayerfully consider which church God wants you to submit to and then make a long-term commitment to that church and its leadership so that you can be equipped and mentored. Doing so is a part of being in submission to God. People who cannot submit to earthly leaders may discover that they are unable to submit to God. But make sure you are growing in a local church environment that allows the anointing to flow freely.

Mentoring involves a relationship in which one person helps develop and empower another.

Younger Christians need models of spiritual maturity. If they want to grow spiritually, they will profit immensely from being able to rub shoulders with people who have Godly character and who have built a lifestyle centered on serving the Lord. Having seasoned persons investing in your life will pay huge dividends in your development. It is important to take the initiative to build long-lasting relationships with those that can impart wisdom, knowledge, and experience into your life.

A good mentor can help you grow in your gifting. This could be a pastor in your local church or a mature person who functions in the anointing.

Anything you are going to go through has been experienced by someone else. The best teachers are those who are not afraid to share their own experiences and failures. Learn from others who are gifted and experienced in your area of ministry. They have a wealth of knowledge, wisdom, and experience to impart to you.

3. Build the right relationships

Relationships are important and the people we choose to surround ourselves with should be done with much prayer and consideration. It is important to surround ourselves with people who are like-minded and who love the Lord and who encourage us to pursue and fulfill our calling.

The enemy will try his best to corrupt the good relationship we have with other brothers and sisters in the Lord. We need to do everything possible to preserve the righteous relationships we have, especially with those who build spiritual values into our lives. This includes the relationship with our church and spiritual leaders.

We need to look after our marriages and make sure that it is protected and maintained. We need to encourage our children so that they can grow in their relationship with the Lord. It is our responsibility to prepare the next generation to love the Lord and to be full of faith.

It is important to look after our children and to ensure that they are not caught up in the world. Our children will fulfill our own Godly purpose one day so be aware that the devil will try and corrupt them with temptation and sin.

Proverbs 22:6 - Train up a child in the way he should go, And when he is old he will not depart from it.

There are people that do not belong in our lives and we should consider putting distance between ourselves and them, especially if they are not Godly.

2 Corinthians 6:14 - Do not be unequally yoked together with unbelievers. For what fellowship has righteousness with lawlessness? And what communion has light with darkness?

4. Spend time in prayer

Develop an honest prayer life. Make sure you spend time praying in tongues. In order to grow in the anointing, you need to grow in intimacy with God. Without revelation knowledge, it is not possible to grow. God is all-knowing and will reveal His secrets to those who seek His presence and desire to learn to know Him more and more.

Daniel 11:32 - The people who know their God shall be strong and carry out great exploits.

Intimacy with God is an essential key to preparing ourselves in these last days. It is only as we draw closer and closer to Him each day that we will begin to hear His leading. That is why it is important to have a passion for prayer.

The more you spend time alone with God in prayer, the more sensitive you will be to the voice of God and to distinguish His voice from other voices that deceive and confuse. You will be able to recognize the distinctiveness of the voice of God when it comes. Spend time listening to God and develop your spiritual ear.

Christians who do not spend time in prayer will not grow in their relationship with God. Make sure you have a secure place to pray where you can isolate yourself without any hindrances.

Continually pray for guidance and strength in the use of your spiritual gift and ask God to open your eyes to the needs of others that your gift might reveal. Pray specifically for the meetings and ask God to use you so that you can be a blessing to others. Every meeting has a spiritual theme and purpose that needs to be interpreted. Not every meeting is the same and if you are leading the service, pray and ask God to give you the spiritual key that will unlock God's purposes for that particular program.

Spend time praying in tongues. Speaking in tongues is a lifestyle that should be practiced often. It should be present in your daily devotions and prayer. It is definitely not a once off experience but something that must be engaged in willfully and obediently every day. It should always form part of your daily prayer routine.

1 Corinthians 14:2 - But he who speaks in a tongue does not speak to men but to God, for no-one understands him; however, in the spirit he speaks mysteries.

The mysteries of God are hidden in the Spirit realm and all prophetic secrets are communicated through God's Spirit to your spirit. Praying in tongues enhances this channel of communication.

We are engaged in an invisible war with Satan and we need to be able to engage successfully in spiritual warfare and to discern the spiritual atmosphere.

Believers who grow and excel in the anointing must understand spiritual warfare and know how to expose the demonic assignments of the devil. Intimacy with God becomes a way to engage in spiritual warfare. Whenever a person pursues intimacy they are engaging in spiritual warfare.

Prayer releases the power of God against the principalities and powers in the atmosphere as well as in the physical realm. A healthy prayer life destroys strongholds that demons may have in the lives and in the hearts of God's people. Without prayer there can be no freedom from spiritual afflictions. Praying with the Spirit or in tongues is a powerful and effective defense against the plans and purposes of the enemy. Include a time of praise and worship during your prayer time.

We have been given three swords to subdue the devil. These are the sword of the Spirit, the sword of the Word, and the sword of praise.

Psalm 115:17 - The dead do not praise the Lord.

You will know if you are spiritually dead or not by your praise. Praise is the best sacrifice that we can offer to God.

Worship is not something that only happens in church but involves everything we do and everything we possess.

Spend time worshipping and praising God. God inhabits the praises of His people. Once you position yourself in praise and worship, God will release His supernatural power that will cause the enemy to be confused and defeated.

5. Walk in the Spirit

God lives in the realm of the Spirit. When we walk in the Spirit, we are able to translate ourselves from the natural environment into the environment of the Spirit which is the realm of God's presence.

A key to Christian growth is walking in the Spirit. This enables Christians to grow to maturity and to overcome the desires and temptations of the flesh. But you cannot walk in the Spirit without being baptized with the Spirit.

Galatians 5:16-18 - I say then: Walk in the Spirit, and you shall not fulfill the lust of the flesh. For the flesh lusts against the Spirit and the Spirit against the flesh; and these are contrary to one another, so that you do not do the things that you wish. But if you are led by the Spirit, you are not under the law.

The key to a successful Christian life is walking and living in the anointing of the Holy Spirit. Walking in the Spirit means walking in step with God's plans and purposes and anyone who walk in the flesh walks out of step with God.

The faithful Christian life is a life lived under the direction and by the power of the Spirit. To walk in the Spirit or to be led by the Spirit means to be filled continually with the Spirit of God, to listen to His voice, to discern His will, and to follow His guidance.

When believers walk in the Spirit, the flesh is treated as dead and they cannot be occupied at the same time with Christ and with sin.

These two opposite behaviors are mutually exclusive, so that at all times the believer is either walking in the Spirit or functioning in fleshly desires, but never both at the same time.

Walking in the Spirit is not simply a matter of passive surrender. The Spirit-led life is a life of conflict because it is in constant combat with the old ways of the flesh that continue to tempt and seduce the believer.

Holiness means being set apart from the normal. It also speaks of a purity that allows God to inhabit the temple within each believer.

When a person is saved and filled with the Spirit of God their life belongs to God. In order for the power of God to flow in and through a person, they should walk in a way pleasing to the Lord, which includes living a life of holiness.

The outpouring of the Spirit is definitely not a once off experience but something that must be engaged in willfully and obediently every day. It should always form part of our daily prayer routine. We must continue to walk in the Spirit and to be filled continually with the Spirit.

This lifestyle generates an increasing thirst for more and more of our innermost being to be filled with the Holy Spirit and we have an infinite capacity within us to accommodate as much of the Holy Spirit as we want.

God gave us His Spirit to help us, to empower us, and to enable us. We cannot be effective without God's Spirit.

Both the fruit and the gifts are essential and are manifestations of the indwelling Spirit. The Holy Spirit produces fruit and these are virtues that demonstrate Jesus' righteousness in the lives of His disciples.

Spiritual growth is a life-long process of manifesting the acts of the flesh less and less and producing the fruit of the Spirit more and more. The Holy Spirit produces fruit in the lives of those who submit to the leading and guidance of the Holy Spirit.

It is only possible to change through the power of the Holy Spirit within us. Any other attempts to effect change are very difficult and seldom long lasting.

2 Corinthians 4:7 - But we have this treasure in earthen vessels, that the excellency of the power may be of God, and not of us.

God places His power in our weak earthen vessels and it is that power that is released. Without this power, we are weak vessels. We cannot achieve effective ministry in the flesh.

The evidence of God's power within us is the fruit of the Spirit. That is totally opposite to the old nature. God's power is able to change our old ways. Christians should change. We should display the nature and character of Jesus or else we are no different to the world. We cannot change in our own strength – only through God's power within us.

The Spirit-filled life is an obedient and abiding life and God's people are encouraged to be continually filled with the Spirit in order to maintain their spiritual walk and growth.

6. Stay fresh

When God touches you with His Spirit heaven touches you and when heaven touches you, all the blessings of heaven touch you. These blessings include healing and health, happy relationships, success, prosperity, ministry, and so much more.

When heaven touches earth, things change everywhere and our living environment changes. God's people live in a different environment to those in the world, even though we all live on earth. That is why we need to allow streams of fresh flowing waters from the throne of God to flow over us so that times of refreshing can come.

We are on a spiritual journey and the journey can get tough. We are exposed to pressure, opposition, obstacles, demonic strategies, and so many other negative things that can take us off course.

We need the Spirit of God to refresh us. Many Christians are going to give up especially in the last days because they will begin to feel the heat. They are going give up in the last leg of the journey and they are going to throw in the towel and walk away from God and from their purpose.

Acts 3:19 - Repent therefore and be converted, that your sins may be blotted out, so that times of refreshing may come from the presence of the Lord.

These words were spoken by Peter and he was someone who really struggled with his walk with the Lord. He saw all the signs and wonders that Jesus performed but yet he wondered whether Jesus was the Christ. At the crucifixion, Peter denied Jesus because he never ever had a spiritual revelation of Jesus until his baptism in the Spirit at Pentecost when the Spirit of God came upon him and changed him. It is only the Spirit of God that can bring revelation, change, revival, and refreshing so that we can do extraordinary things for God.

The baptism in the Holy Spirit not only empowered Peter for supernatural ministry, but it also refreshed him and made his spiritual journey bearable. So many people give up because they try to do things in their own power. For Peter, the anointing represented new opportunities and a chance to start again. Peter experienced many low points in his life and welcomed the refreshing that the wind of the Spirit brought on him. He was touched by heaven and became a new person. He never was the same again.

I believe that revival is coming, but the church is desperately in need of a refreshing before revival. I believe a sifting is coming before revival. Trials and temptations are going to come. Revival is coming and God wants us to stay refreshed in body, mind, and spirit. Today there are too many Christians who have given up and walked away from their purpose. We need to open up a door of refreshing that comes into the house and prepares us for the revival fire.

We all consist of body, soul, and spirit and we can get sick in anyone of those three areas. We can get sick in our bodies. Refreshing can come upon your body through the healing anointing.

It is a refreshing that comes from the cross which can allow you to experience health and healing. We often speak about revival, but our bodies also need a revival.

We can also become sick in our minds. Old thinking patterns can return and torment us. But God can revive and refresh our minds with His Word so that we can be renewed in our thinking.

There are many examples of God's people who became sick in their spirits. What are the symptoms of you being sick in your spirit? It brings feelings of hopelessness and you stop caring. You find yourself at a point in your life when you no longer feel like praying and you feel disconnected from everything and everyone. You can have a sense of extreme loneliness even though there are people around you. This is an indication that you need a refreshing from heaven.

The devil knows that you have a supernatural purpose and that God has called you for something great and powerful. He will make sure that you become tired, that your attitude towards your destiny will change, and that you are harassed and tormented. But do not allow him to deceive you because it will bring death to your vision.

You are the vehicle that God wants to use to touch other people and if that vehicle is broken, people will not receive what God wants for them.

7. Grow in the anointing

2 Corinthians 3:17-18 - Now the Lord is that Spirit: and where the Spirit of the Lord is, there is liberty. But we all, with open face beholding as in a glass the glory of the Lord, are changed into the same image from glory to glory, even as by the Spirit of the Lord.

Every born-again, Spirit-filled child of God has the anointing upon their life. However, we are responsible for keeping and increasing the level of the anointing upon our lives. That is why some walk in a greater anointing than others.

The Word teaches us to be continually filled with God's Spirit to ensure a fresh outflow of the anointing.

The highest attainable level of God's anointing is represented by the waters that flow from God's throne to individuals, groups, or nations and wherever these waters go, they bring healing and life to the needy.

We have rivers of living water flowing from our innermost being. Because we are the New Testament temples of the Holy Spirit, we are the source of God's river.

From the time Samuel the prophet anointed David, he grew in the anointing, authority, and influence. He was anointed as king of Israel, but did not become king until twenty years later.

We need to understand this process. So many Christians become discouraged and walk away from God's plan for their lives, because they want to fulfill their ministry immediately and minister in the full power of the anointing. That seldom happens. There is normally a slow process that God has for us to follow until He releases us into our full potential.

While you are growing in the things of God, be faithful in the small things as you learn to exercise your gift. That is what David did. He used his anointing to kill the lion and the bear. God first tests believers with small things before they are promoted.

It is important to go beyond your initial empowerment and to develop a continuous relationship and intimacy with the Holy Spirit. We should develop in the anointing by degrees. Experiences in the anointing are progressive steps to higher levels.

There are principles to follow so that we can be ready for an increased anointing. It starts with the first measure of anointing God places on our lives. There must be testing and we must prove ourselves faithful. The increase and operation depends on us and not on God. It is our responsibility to grow into our anointing. Just as we grow from faith to faith, from glory to glory, and from grace to grace, so do we also grow in the anointing.

8. Grow in your gift

Every Christian is:

- Created for ministry
- Needed for ministry
- Called into ministry

- Empowered for ministry
- Gifted for ministry

God gives natural talents to all people. He also gives spiritual gifts to believers by His Holy Spirit and through His Son.

Both talents and gifts can be used for the glory of God, but spiritual gifts are supernatural abilities given to believers for building up the church. God has given the gifts because the church cannot be equipped and built with natural talents. Each one of us must discover our spiritual gift.

Many churches do not have these gifts operating in their meetings because they do not give the Holy Spirit a chance to speak to the congregation.

Spiritual gifts are special abilities the Holy Spirit gives to the followers of Jesus to build the body of Christ and to make the church effective in ministry.

Matthew 16:18 - And I also say to you that you are Peter, and on this rock I will build My church, and the gates of Hades shall not prevail against it.

Building the church is something in which the Lord Jesus is directly involved and which is an operation of Holy Spirit. The church was birthed on the day of Pentecost with the outpouring of the Holy Spirit.

In the church today, we find many people who are not baptized in the Holy Spirit and think that it is not necessary to be filled with the Spirit. But the Word of God teaches us that baptism in the Holy Spirit precedes ministry.

The baptism of the Holy Spirit was given to empower ordinary believers for supernatural ability and to equip the church with spiritual gifts and ministries.

Acts 1:8 - But you shall receive power when the Holy Spirit has come upon you; and you shall be witnesses to Me in Jerusalem, and in all Judea and Samaria, and to the end of the earth.

A spiritual gift is an expression of the Holy Spirit in the life of believers which empowers them to serve the body of Christ, the church.

God has sovereignly and variously equipped each member to function in his or her unique place in the body. This function is not optional but expected and essential to the body as a whole. And while no one gift is universal, all within the body are to care for the others in every way possible. This is God's way of ministering to His church, not through a gifted pastor only, but through all the members gifted to serve one another. This is the only way a body can function.

The most significant gift Christ has given His church is the Holy Spirit. No gift is more important for Christ's followers today.

Paul was speaking of different ways of ministering, or using, these gifts. In other words, two people could have the same gift yet minister or use it differently. There is plenty of room for different ways of ministering the same gift, but it is the same Lord controlling them all. Therefore, they must conform to these guidelines that Paul was giving.

He mentioned that different people in the body of Christ have different positions or functions.

Spiritual gifts can be quenched through sin, neglect, and laziness. We need to be continually filled with God's Spirit and cultivate a hunger for spiritual gifts. God wants us to stir up and grow into that which He has freely given to us so that we can maximize our effectiveness in the body of Christ. We have a responsibility to develop our spiritual gift and to grow in our anointing by means of learning, training, and practice for the benefit of the local church and other believers.

We need to invest our gifts wisely in order to reach our highest potential and fulfill our destiny and ministry calling.

1 Timothy 4:14-15 - Do not neglect your gift, which was given you through a prophetic message when the body of elders laid their hands on you. Be diligent in these matters; give yourself wholly to them, so that everyone may see your progress.

9. Do not waste your time

So many Christians are busy running everywhere but never really settle down. They live their lives trying so many things and if those things do not work out, they try something else. After a lifetime of fruitless searching, the best years of their lives have been wasted. They live their life by experiment instead of by purpose.

We are all called by God. It is therefore important to find out from God what that call is. Find out where God wants you to live. Find out who He wants you to marry. Find out what He wants you to spend the rest of your life doing.

It takes time and effort to build something that lasts. It does not happen overnight. God gives us a few decades on earth and we should use that time producing fruit. We should use that time wisely and build equity for the Kingdom of God. If your life is drifting by aimlessly, something is wrong. Boredom is a good indication that something big is missing in your walk with God.

Depending on your call and ministry, God will place you under the authority of a pastor or a spiritual leader. Generally, God will not move you around. If you have moved to two or three churches in the past few years, there is something wrong. If you have moved out because of problems with the church leaders, you may need to be honest with yourself and find out why these problems persist.

You will probably never fulfill your God-given purpose unless you settle down and allow God to prepare you for your future. God has not placed you on this earth to live and die. Every step you take should be directed towards your spiritual goal. Do not take one step unless it is going to produce something positive.

10. Deal with personal issues

a. Allow God to do the restoring and the renewing

We go through things and we need people to help us, but ultimately it is always going to be between you and God and He wants you to discuss your issues with Him.

He wants you to be open and honest about your situation and He is one person you can speak to. When we do that, restoration can take place.

David went through a lot of personal struggles and he always let God know what he was going through. This mostly comes from the past and there are so many people who are tormented by guilt. But God wants us to have a new beginning.

He does not want us to be stuck with baggage that has come from a place from where we have moved on.

Psalm 51:12 - Restore unto me the joy of Your salvation, And uphold me by Your generous Spirit.

Why would David pray this prayer? It must have been because he lost his joy. He was going through emotional struggles and hurts and needed to be restored.

Psalm 51:10 - Create in me a clean heart, O God, And renew a right spirit within me.

This is great prayer to pray in stressful times. Be refreshed and renewed and drink of the waters that flow from God's throne.

b. Be patient

John 5:5 - Now a certain man was there who had an infirmity thirty eight years.

Many of God's children lose their place in His Kingdom because they become impatient.

This man waited for thirty eight long years and is a reflection on our future and destiny. Although things may take a long time to manifest in your life, be patient because it will come to pass.

You might have been waiting for many years, but do not give up on your miracle.

The lame man did not leave that place. That speaks about being in the right place. This can also mean serving in a church or ministry. You could be in the same position in your church for years. Maybe some people have told you to leave and find another place of worship, but God always rewards patience and faithfulness. God is about to visit you and give you favor and use you for mighty things.

When Samuel anointed David King over Israel, it took twenty years for that prophecy to come to pass. Many people have given up on their purpose because they have not understood God's timing. God is not in a hurry. He takes His time when it comes to fulfilling prophecies.

Just relax, be patient, and stay on fire for God. Do not try to help God in any way. He does not need your help. You will only mess things up for yourself and others.

Whatever He promised will come to pass in His time. In the meantime stay faithful to your church and your worship so that when the time comes you are not backslidden. When your time comes to pass, you need to be in relationship with God in order to fulfill your purpose.

c. Allow God to mold and make you

Isaiah 64:8 - But now, O LORD, You are our Father; We are the clay, and You our potter; And all we are the work of Your hand.

Let God remold you and reprogram you and rebuild the things that you have built in the flesh. This can be a painful process, but allow God to start rebuilding something beautiful through His Spirit.

d. Deal with your weaknesses

1 Corinthians 10:13 - No temptation has overtaken you except such as is common to man; but God is faithful, who will not allow you to be tempted beyond what you are able, but with the temptation will also make the way of escape, that you may be able to bear it.

We all have strengths and weaknesses and we need to deal with our weaknesses if we are to be used by God.

As you start growing in the things of God and as you start dealing with issues, you will discover your strengths, but you will also discover your weaknesses.

You will never ever fulfill your destiny unless you deal with your weakest point. For example, you may be strong in the Word, strong in witnessing to others, strong in commitment to your local church, casting out demons, etc., but you must know and understand that the one thing that will limit you is your weakness. We all have weaknesses and we should be aware of those weaknesses, because that is the point where the devil causes us to fail and not our strong points.

Over the years, David grew in the anointing and performed supernatural things, eventually reigning as king over the whole of Israel.

But he never dealt with his weakness, which was his love for other women, and it destroyed his reputation. If David had dealt with his weakness he would have fulfilled his potential. His weakness kept him back which indirectly caused him to be disqualified from building God's temple.

Now God will still love you but you will not be able to put that full distance between you and the devil if you have not dealt with your weaknesses.

The second aspect of salvation relates to born again believers maintaining their salvation by living a life of holiness and bearing good fruit.

Philippians 2:12 - Therefore, my beloved, as you have always obeyed, not as in my presence only, but now much more in my absence, work out your own salvation with fear and trembling.

It is also very important for the children of God to be part of a local church. The objective in going to church is to build a relationship with God and others. The Christian life is not always an easy road. It is so easy to become discouraged. When believers separate themselves from other believers they become vulnerable and are an easy target for the devil. Never before have people been confronted with so many voices and so many choices. God speaks to His people as a whole and He speaks to them individually, guiding them into truth and reminding them what is right and warning them what is wrong. His is a voice that tells the truth when so many other voices cannot be trusted.

e. Repent

Sin and compromise will destroy your future with God. God wants all of you but will want you to give everything to Him willingly and obediently.

A lukewarm carnal spirit has invaded the church and it is so easy to drop your guard and lower your standard.

On-going sin in a person's life is an open invitation to demons. Yielding to sin is yielding to the devil. Repentance is a firm resolve in the Lord to forsake sin, to turn around, and to walk in the ways of God.

Romans 6:16 - Do you not know that to whom you present yourselves slaves to obey, you are that one's slaves whom you obey, whether of sin to death, or of obedience to righteousness.

Essential to growing closer to God in faith, devotion, and love is to repent of those behaviors, desires, beliefs, and ideas that are sinful. Repentance involves more than merely turning away from sin. By repenting a person must also renounce everything that opposes God and all that He finds sinful. This includes renouncing Satan and his ways and renouncing personal sins.

Walk continually in the Spirit and do not walk out of step with God by walking in the flesh. Make wise choices and changes in your life and you will see how God will begin to bless you and use you for His plans and purposes.

Romans 10:15 - And how shall they preach unless they are sent? As it is written: "How beautiful are the feet of those who preach the gospel of peace, who bring glad tidings of good things!"

God formed Adam from the dust of the earth. We are imperfect vessels and have so many weaknesses. But God created each one of us special and unique. He has good plans for our lives. God's hands were upon us when we were in our mother's womb and He has never stopped forming us.

We are all different because we have different assignments. Do not try to be someone else because when God's fingers shaped you in your mother's womb, He formed you so that you could perform a unique function.

But you need to know that the hands of God are still on your life and He has never stopped forming you.

Philippians 1:6 - Being confident of this very thing, that He who has begun a good work in you will complete it until the day of Jesus Christ

Whatever God makes is beautiful and wonderful. God may take a long time but be patient and allow God to take that time in your life because He is perfecting that which concerns Him.

Sometimes we believe that we have to work very hard in order to please God. But God knows that you are never going to come up to His standard on your own. If you will allow God to do a work in your life, you will not have to work so hard trying to please Him.

God has given the New Testament church anointed leaders that help Him to form Christ in each of us. He is still forming your mouth, your ears, your feet, etc., until Christ is fully formed in you. It is a process and it takes time.

God bless you as you position yourself for God's plans and purposes for your life and for the nations.

Author

Dr. Jeff van Wyk is the President of Team Impact Christian University, USA

Contact Details:

5536 Superior Drive Suite D
Baton Rouge, LA70816
USA

Tel: 1 225 292 1771

www.joyministries.com
www.tiuniversity.com
www.jeffvanwyk.com

Books by Dr. Jeff van Wyk

1. The Five-Fold Anointing
2. Learning to Lead in Ministry
3. Christian Ethics
4. The Five-Fold Prayer
5. Spiritual Battlefields
6. The Prophetic Anointing
7. All roads lead to Rome. NOT!
8. Millions God's Way
9. Reach
10. Supernatural Gifts
11. Anointed to do Business
12. The Apostolic Anointing
13. Anointed for Ministry

Whether you are searching for a Bible College, Christian University, Theological Seminary or Christian College, you have come to the right place!

Team Impact Christian University is an accredited online Christian learning facility that caters for all levels of anointed Christian study.

Team Impact Christian University

The house-hold name in ministry training

www.tiuniversity.com

10296361R00122

Made in the USA
San Bernardino, CA
10 April 2014